The Lyric Speakers
of Old English Poetry

The Lyric Speakers of Old English Poetry

Lois Bragg

Rutherford • Madison • Teaneck
Fairleigh Dickinson University Press
London and Toronto: Associated University Presses

Associated University Presses
440 Forsgate Drive
Cranbury, NJ 08512

Associated University Presses
25 Sicilian Avenue
London WC1A 2QH, England

Associated University Presses
P.O. Box 39, Clarkson Pstl. Stn.
Mississauga, Ontario,
L5J 3X9 Canada

The paper used in this publication meets the requirements
of the American National Standard for Permanence of Paper
for Printed Library Materials Z39.48-1984.

Library of Congress Cataloging-in-Publication Data

Bragg, Lois, 1951–
    The lyric speakers of Old English poetry / Lois Bragg.
        p.   cm.
    Includes bibliographical references and index.
    ISBN 0-8386-3403-6 (alk. paper)
    1. English poetry—Old English, ca. 450–1100—History and criticism.   2. Lyric poetry—History and criticism.   3. Reader -response criticism.   4. Persona (Literature)   I. Title.
    PR210.B7   1991
    829'.1—dc20   89-46414
                                                                        CIP

"Museum Piece" from *Ceremony and Other Poems,* copyright 1950 and renewed 1978 by Richard Wilbur, reprinted by permission of Harcourt Brace Jovanovich, Inc.

Lois me wrat for þæm leofostum manna

Annan • Carle • Claran • Ruþe

7 eallra swiðost for Olgan

Contents

Preface   9

Part I: Groundwork

1. Meanwhile, a Millennium Later . . .   15
   The Lyric Poem   19
   Oral, Manuscript, and Print Cultures   24
   Poet and Audience   29
   The Lyric Speaker   36

Part II: The Poems

2. The Inanimate Speaker   43
3. The Adoptable Speaker   58
4. The Nonpersonal Speaker   65
5. The Fictive Speaker   85
6. The Personal Speaker   112
7. Two Masterpieces   121

Afterword   136
Notes   139
Works Cited   148
Index   157

Preface

This book is an investigation of a wonder: the possibility of communication and empathic identification across a millennium through a handful of often obscure and pervasively alien lyric poems. My topic is the thirty-some extant Old English lyrics, of which only a half dozen or so have any reputation outside the small circle of persons who are functionally literate in the vernacular of the Anglo-Saxons. What I am attempting here is to establish the reader's privilege to define for herself a literary corpus and to organize her thinking about the poems it comprises in ways that cut through traditional critical conventions. For example, others have complained about the use of the term "elegy" in Old English scholarship, but we have all kept on using it anyway in a kind of perpetual game of "Dun is in the myre." It is one of my hopes for this book that it will contribute to the speedy demise of this tired concept and thus open the way for additional fresh juxtapositions of the poems and the fresh readings that will follow.

Part I provides the critical groundwork for the readings, including discussions of the lyric genre, of literacy and orality, and of the relations among audience, poet, and poem, all of which suggest that the lyric speaker is of paramount importance for our understanding and enjoyment of these lyrics. Part I is essential, and should be read first; thereafter, the reader is invited to wander at will among the chapters of part II, each of which discusses a type of Old English lyric speaker and the poems that employ that speaker. In these pages, the reader will find discussions of prayers, riddles, and charms, Cynewulf's epilogues, the poems of *The Anglo-Saxon Chronicle,* lyric interludes from *Beowulf,* and many more in addition to the so-called elegies. Finding that the Cross in "The Dream of the Rood" behaves very much like the speaking books in certain amateurishly versified manuscript prefaces may be on the level of finding that a fish is symmetrical, and that is perhaps why no one ever thought much about it before, in print anyway. I, for one, found this discovery to be enormously helpful in making sense of "The Dream of the Rood" and "The Husband's Message." When the latter is separated from "The Wife's Lament" and other "elegies" (to which it has become attached for no good reason since it meets

9

no one's definition of the elegy) its playfulness comes to life. Reading "The Battle of Brunanburh" with its companion pieces in *The Anglo-Saxon Chronicle* (all of which have similar speakers) rather than with "The Battle of Maldon" as is de rigueur, fills one with admiration for its rhetorical techniques and sets up intriguing questions about the role of literature in Anglo-Saxon political propaganda, which I hope someone will attempt to answer. And so it has seemed to me throughout. Grouping the lyrics according to the kind of speaker they employ is surely arbitrary, but no more arbitrary than the traditional categories newly valorized by Greenfield and Calder in their *New Critical History*, and, in many cases, somewhat more productive. Several months into my work, something happened that convinced me I was doing something right. Two poems perversely refused to stay where I thought they should be, reread and rethink as I might. The funny thing was that those two poems were the very two I had always taken for works of genius: "The Dream of the Rood" and "The Wanderer." Discussions of these two poems are thus reserved for the last chapter, which alone assumes the reader's acquaintance with the previous chapters of part II.

This book owes a great deal to my family (who are named in the dedication) and to a host of friends, acquaintances, teachers, and colleagues who encouraged me in one way or another—people like my ninth-grade English teacher Mrs. Kirk, for instance, who thought I had a talent for the classics (I don't think she had Classical West Saxon in mind, though) or like Helen Bennett, who turns ordinary Old English conference sessions into epiphanies. Among those whom I thank for *intentional* help with this book are F. Anne Payne, Robert Edwards, Ann Haskell, and Daniel G. Calder, who read the dissertation that started this book and who offered good suggestions for improvement; Theresa Covley, whose concept of what a librarian can do for a patron knows no bounds; Emily Jensen, William Woods, and Michael Dunne, who read and commented on various sections of the typescript from the vantage points of their various areas of expertise (Old English, rhetoric, and Hawthorne, respectively); Derek Pearsall, who read the entire next-to-last draft and whose kindness encouraged me at a particularly low point; and Bruce White, who read the page proofs and index, and saved me from many embarrassing errors. I thank you all.

All quotations from Old English poems and all Modern English titles are from *The Anglo-Saxon Poetic Records*, edited by G. P. Krapp and E. V. K. Dobbie, unless otherwise indicated. All citations from their notes or introductory material use the abbreviation *ASPR*, followed by volume and page numbers. Translations, unless otherwise indicated, are my own.

The Lyric Speakers
of Old English Poetry

Part I
Groundwork

1
Meanwhile, a Millennium Later . . .

Works of art are shipped like coal from the Ruhr and logs from the Black Forest. During the First World War Hölderlin's hymns were packed in the soldier's knapsack together with cleaning gear. Beethoven's quartets lie in the storerooms of the publishing house like potatoes in a cellar.

Thus wrote Heidegger on the "thingly aspect" of works of art (19). Certainly works of art must have a thingly aspect: Höderlin's hymns could not be read nor Beethoven's quartets played unless their texts were printed and distributed. Most of us, however, know that a work of art has some essential existence apart from its thingliness, although we often act as if it doesn't. Consider this poem by Richard Wilbur:

MUSEUM PIECE

The good grey guardians of art
Patrol the halls on spongy shoes,
Impartially protective, though
Perhaps suspicious of Toulouse.

Here dozes one against the wall,
Disposed upon a funeral chair.
A Degas dancer pirouettes
Upon the parting of his hair.

See how she spins! The grace is there,
But strain as well is plain to see.
Degas loved the two together:
Beauty joined to energy.

Edgar Degas purchased once
A fine El Greco, which he kept
Against the wall beside his bed
To hang his pants on while he slept.

The museum visitor who is the speaker of this poem experiences a painting of a ballerina in its "work-aspect": "See how she spins!" he exclaims of what is merely a static though valuable object for the museum guard asleep beneath it—or her. The speaker is fortunate in his experience, for collected works of bygone eras tend to remain obstinately in their thingliness. Heidegger writes: "World-with-drawal and world-decay can never be undone. The works are no longer the same as they once were. It is they themselves, to be sure, that we encounter there, but they themselves are gone by. As bygone works they stand over against us in the realm of tradition and conservation. Henceforth they remain merely such objects" (41). For Degas, in Wilbur's poem, the painting by El Greco belonged to a world three hundred years gone by, in the realm of tradition, and, hence, an object, happily suitable as a clothes tree.

We hypostatize works of art not only because their worlds are bygone, but also because we live in "the age of mechanical reproduction," to use Walter Benjamin's label. Reproductions, Benjamin writes, lack "presence in time and space" (222). Right now, I am sitting at my desk in a concrete-block room in Tennessee. In front of me, pinned to a bulletin board, is a postcard, a print of a seventeenth-century Flemish painting of St. Matthew writing the gospel as it is dictated to him by an angel. On my tape player is Mozart's Requiem Mass. When I get tired of the Requiem, which I tend to play over and over, I'll get up and put on another tape. Or if I get a telephone call, I'll turn it off. If I ever lose my profound belief in the superhuman inspiration of works of art, which is the reason I bought the postcard and keep it in front of me, I'll throw it away—I paid only a quarter for it. The tape and the postcard are merely reproductions, objects available for my manipulation and disposal according to my whim. They lack a presence of their own, the kind of presence that would prevent me from walking out of a performance of the Requiem Mass—let alone an actual requiem mass. Yet because we in the twentieth century experience works of art chiefly by means of reproductions, we are not in the habit of perceiving the presence of the work of art, its work aspect. In an art museum—and here the problem is compounded by the art having been removed from its world—we breeze through the rooms looking around as though we were in a furniture showroom shopping for a new couch, and many of us do in fact walk out of concerts. Why not? Why spend a sunny Sunday afternoon listening to the Requiem Mass when you can get it on tape and hear it that evening while you are typing up some notes?

Another kind of reproduction that I own and use is a set of six books, uniformly sized and printed and bound in green cloth: *The Anglo-Saxon Poetic Records.* More than half of the contents of each volume consists of the editors' commentary, and much of that commentary consists of references to other scholarly commentary, all of which can be duly found in physical form at any large university library. The remaining pages of each volume contain printed editions of the exant "poetic records," verse discourse discovered in manuscripts that are now housed in museums. Each poem is titled by the editors and provided with modern punctuation and a variety of textual emendations, the purpose of which is to make the poems make sense to twentieth-century college professors in those spots in which the manuscripts refuse to do so. The texts of the poems are also broken into lines, so they look just like modern poems and not at all like their exemplars in the manuscripts. My *ASPR* sits on a shelf above my word processor with other objects that I use when I use it: the Clark Hall dictionary, the Bessinger and Smith concordance, Mitchell's *Old English Syntax,* a three-ring binder containing my translations, two shoe boxes full of index cards, boxes of floppy disks, pencils, and teacups. I sit down at my well-lighted desk in the waning years of the twentieth century, open Volume III, the Exeter Book, scan the table of contents for the text of the poem I want to study, pick up a Papermate Sharpwriter pencil, and read aloud a language that is not my mother tongue, nor the mother tongue of any living person. And then something happens. The inert object stirs. The language starts to present itself to me as though it actually were my mother tongue. The poem emerges from its thingliness and struggles into being: "Wulf, min Wulf, wena me þine seoce gedydon, þine seldcymas, murnende mod, nales meteliste." Yes, I know. I know what it is like to long for an absent loved one with a troubled mind, to feel oneself become physically ill, to try to explain to others that it is not lack of food that is wasting me away, but his "seldom-comings." Or perhaps I turn to another page and read: "Forþon nu min hyge hweorfeð ofer hreþerlocan, min modsefa mid mereflode ofer hwæles eþel hweorfeð wide, eorþan sceatas, cymeð eft to me gifre and grædig, gielleð anfloga, hweteð on hwælweg hreþer unwearnum ofer holma gelagu." And I know that, too. I, too, have found my thought turning about in the filing cabinets of my mind and heart, escaping to fly over the sea and returning to me "ravenous and greedy," inciting me irresistibly to follow it with my physical body, although I have no wings.

How is it possible that a thousand-year-poem, a sequence of words in a dead language miraculously preserved and then ruthlessly edited, causes me to recollect what I know of the human experience, the things I know but have forgotten because I've filed them away in order to grade freshman essays or walk my children to their music lessons? The lines I have quoted are presented to me in a context foreign to their world. They come to me as printed discourse, something to be studied, something collected, something preserved: an object. Even if I were to go to Exeter and read the manuscript in the cathedral library, their world is gone. Even if I were somehow to conjure myself back into eleventh-century Exeter, like a Doctor Faustus, what ever would I be able to say to Bishop Leofric about the *mycel englisc boc*? And what would I be able to understand about it from him? As Paul Zumthor writes, medieval texts come from a universe "in which we by no means participate. Any analogy between that universe and ours must be supposed illusory (until there is explicit proof of the contrary), which does not mean that pertinent analogies do not exist" (29). At this point in my wandering thoughts, I wonder how one can ever discover what those pertinent analogies might be (even though I have just in fact observed two of them: the longing for a loved one and the birdlike nature of thought). For example, the passage quoted above about the speaker's thoughts escaping and returning begins with the word *forþon,* an adverb whose meaning is unknown to me, and, I suspect, to all other persons now living. I can stop reading and research the word. And when I do, the poem is gone; it had returned to its thingliness, to printed words that resist my prying. Heidegger makes an analogy with color: "Color shines and wants only to shine. When we analyze it in rational terms by measuring its wavelengths, it is gone. It shows itself only when it remains undisclosed and unexplained" (47). All this is not to say that wavelengths should not be measured or that Old English poems should not be edited, but rather than these activities hypostatize essences, relationships, and events: in short, non-objects. A lyric poem is not an object, but an event. To use Stanley Fish's terms, "[l]iterature is a kinetic art" (43), "the occasion for a temporal experience," even though its physical form presents it to us as a spatial object (345). We confront the edited Old English lyrics as reproduced art objects to be studied and classified and amended and made explicable. Until we begin to *read* them.

At this point the question is, How does an Old English poem *occur* in the face of all tendencies to treat it as an object: the decay of the world in which it was generated, our greater familiarity with reproductions than with productions, and our apparently irresistible desire to manipulate works of verbal art that come to us in

manuscript form? My attempt to answer this question here addresses three issues: 1) how lyric poems in general occur, 2) how
the notion of poetry held by a newly literate manuscript culture
such as Anglo-Saxon England differs from our own notions, and 3)
what both these issues can tell us about the relationship among
poet, audience, speaker, and lyric poem.

The Lyric Poem

Peter Dronke, surely the foremost authority on the medieval
lyric, prefaces his 1968 study with this remark:

> I hope to be forgiven if I do not begin with a discussion or definition of
> the nature of lyric itself. My subject is the contents of the *chansonniers*
> or *Liederhandschriften* of the Middle Ages, in all their diversity, and by
> "lyrical" I shall mean whatever belongs to, or essentially resembles,
> what is contained in these. (*Medieval Lyric* 10)

Daniel Albright, in a recent book on lyricality, writes: "a lyric is
that which resists definition" (viii), and, "sometimes it seems as if
the lyric genre consists of what is left over when all other genres are
subtracted from the corpus of literature" (ix). One is only too
inclined to agree: the lyric genre is notoriously hard to define,
although all of us can identify a lyric poem as such when we read
one.

Behind the attempt to posit the lyric as a genre lies the question
of why anyone would want to do that in the first place. Taxonomies
are not natural, but rather cultural, and the Anglo-Saxons themselves had no word for lyric poetry. Roscoe E. Parker's study of the
three Old English words for *poem* reveals that *sang* can mean
"anything that is sung or chanted" (60); *leoð* may be either "an
aphoristic or lyric poem" (61); and *gyd* may refer to "an elegy,
moral tale, maxim, or parable" (63). Parker's glosses attempt to
match Old English nouns with Modern English generic terms, yet
his study tells us little more than the *gyd* is merely a brief work of
verbal art; *leoð* the same, but in verse only; and *sang,* a *leoð* orally
delivered. A "critical lexicon" such as this is clearly not intended
for making generic distinctions.

Northrop Frye argues that "[t]he purpose of criticism by genres
is not so much to classify as to clarify such traditions and affinities,
thereby bringing out a large number of literary relationships that
would not be noticed as long as there were no context established

for them" (247–48). This seems a worthy motivation, especially in light of the current state of Old English literary studies, which tends to impose many narrowly defined genres, such as the *consolatio,* the *planctus,* the *encomium,* the penitential poem, and the *Frauenlied* on the tiny corpus of extant lyrics, thus obscuring relationships among them.[1] By far the most widely used of such narrow generic terms is the elegy, which Stanley B. Greenfield authoritatively defines as "a relatively short reflective or dramatic poem embodying a contrasting pattern of loss and consolation, ostensibly based upon a specific personal experience or observation, and expressing an attitude towards that experience" ("Old English Elegies" 143). But the "contrasting pattern of loss and consolation" is in fact a distinguishing feature of the bulk of Old English verse of any sort, and the remainder of Greenfield's definition states merely that elegies are lyric poems. Just which poems belong to this genre is everywhere argued. The seven most popular of the eleven possible candidates are "The Ruin," "The Wanderer," "The Seafarer," "Deor," "Wulf and Eadwacer," "The Wife's Lament," and "The Husband's Message"; the other four being "Resignation," "The Riming Poem," and two lyrics from *Beowulf,* "The Last Survivor" (lines 2231–70a) and "The Father's Lament" (2444–62a).[2] As this list demonstrates, the five or seven or nine short poems that most often are included in the genre happen to be those most popular with modern readers, a coincidence that should arouse suspicions of the term's usefulness in distinguishing anything but the taste of modern scholars.

Prosody is often taken to be a distinguishing characteristic of the lyric poem, and it does distinguish the lyric from other kinds of verse literature in some ethnic corpora: classical Greek is the classic example, and modern English is another, since nowadays the lyric is the only kind of literature to be written in verse of any kind. The Middle Ages does provide a few examples of this phenomenon, such as the Mozarabic *muwashshahat* and the Portuguese *cantigas de amigo,* both of which are recognizable by sight—by their appearance in the manuscript—but it was far more common for lyric prosody to be identical to narrative prosody. The lyric poetry of der von Kurenberc, for example, is written in the four-line strophe of the *Nibelungenlied,* and many of Chaucer's "balades" are in the rime royal stanza he used for the *Troilus* and four of the Canterbury tales, or in the eight-line stanza he used for the Monk's tragedies. In the case of Old English poetry, there is, of course, only one system of versification, the alliterative, four-stress line that the Anglo-Saxons used for everything from the epic to the riddle, the homily to the charm, the ridiculous to the sublime.

Tone is a second criterion that is sometimes said to distinguish or define lyric poetry. For example, the wit and playfulness found in the lyric poetry of the *Minnesänger* and *trouveres* finds a true parallel only in the lyrical prefaces to contemporary narratives, not in the narrative poetry proper of those cultures. However, other examples do not come readily to mind. Continental poetry generally shows great variety of tone. The troubadour lyrics, for example—nearly all on unsatisfied love—can be witty, tender, irreverent, bathetic, sarcastic, resigned, or obscene. In Old English poetry we find a much greater uniformity of tone, just as we find a greater uniformity in the prosody. Saint's life and heroic epic, penitential lyric and love lyric, all genres (except the riddles) are marked by great urgency, earnestness, and, in most cases, moral seriousness. In sum, while continental and Middle English literature is diverse in both prosody and tone, Anglo-Saxon literature is remarkably uniform in both, but in few cases can the lyric be distinguished from the non-lyric by verse form or tone.

If we can justify positing a lyric genre on the grounds that it brings poems together rather than dividing them into discrete categories, as Frye argues, we should define it as broadly and inclusively as possible, keeping in mind that we are aiming to define the lyric operationally—that is, as an event—considering formal features only as they relate to how the poem occurs. Roman Jakobson's analysis of the components of the act of communication is useful as a starting point. In any act of verbal communication, there is an addresser and an addressee, a message, a context for that message, a contact and a code through which the message is conveyed (353–57). Jakobson distinguishes six kinds of discourse—each one corresponds to one particular component of communication. Discourse that focuses on the addresser employs the first-person and is termed the emotive mode. Lyric poetry, according to Jakobson's scheme, belongs to the emotive mode. Discourse that focuses on the addressee employs the second person and is termed the conative mode—prayers and charms belong to this category. Discourse that focuses on the context employs the third person and is termed the referential mode. The epic belongs to this category. (The other three components and modes do not concern us here.)

Jakobson's taxonomy makes it clear that narrative and didactic literature refer to a context external to the relationship between addresser and addressee, while lyric poetry, prayers, and charms have in common their occurrence completely within the I–You relationship. In other words, what Jakobson sees as a trichotomy of I–You–It can better be seen as a dichotomy. Emile Benveniste, working strictly from a linguistic standpoint, establishes a crucial distinction between the third person on the one hand and the first and second persons on the other (217–22). While the third person refers to "an 'objective' situation" (221) outside the linguistic act, the first and second persons lack such material reference, for they have meaning only in the act of discourse itself. Benveniste's theory thus offers useful support for seeing I–You as referring to a relationship and It as referring to an objective reality, but it is Martin Buber who shows the profound implications of this dichotomy.

For Buber, our world is twofold in accordance with our two basic word-pairs, I–You and I–It. The I–It world is measurable and manipulable, for it consists of objects that are detached from and alien to every I. The I–You world, on the other hand, has no objects or borders, for it is the world of relations, but it is continually dissolving back into the I–It world of objects. The I–You world is momentary, evanescent. "In this firm and wholesome chronicle [i.e., the It-world] the You-moments appear as queer lyric-dramatic episodes. Their spell may be seductive, but they pull us dangerously to extremes, loosening the well-tried structure, leaving behind more doubt than satisfaction, shaking up our security—altogether uncanny, altogether indispensable" (84–85). This is surely what lyric poetry is: the evanescent, magical verbal art that occurs in the world of relationship, the relationship between the speaker and the reader. The reader of a lyric poem does not confront its speaker as a He, She, or It—a detached and objective being, as the characters of narratives are—but rather as a You, a being who is, for him-, her-, or itself, an *I*.

This is not to say that the lyric genre can include only those works employing the first- or second-person pronouns, although often lyric poetry is said to be distinguished by its "personal" speaker. Of course, it is a commonplace among medievalists that the concept of personal literature is a modern one, an invention of the Romantic era. We know that the medieval concept of self, of the individual distinct from the world and human society, was, if not actually nonexistent, at least not developed to anything near the modern concept of self. Leo Spitzer writes of an obvious but all too often forgotten notion when he distinguishes between the poetic "I" and the empirical "I" of the medieval author. We forget that to mistake the poetic "I" for the poet can occur only in a society that exalts the individual over the universal, and that understands the concept of what Spitzer calls "intellectual property"—that is, our society, not the medieval poet's.

What then do modern scholars mean when they speak of personal poetry in connection with the medieval lyric, as many do? They seem to refer to signed poetry in which the gender of the speaker is the same as that of the poet and in which the topic is something that is nowadays regarded as private, such as sexual relations or religious experience. What is usually left out of discussions of personal poetry is its highly conventional nature, and the fact that personal poetry is usually indistinguishable from contemporary poems written in the voice of the opposite sex (that is, women's lyrics written by men), and from anonymous poetry, and from dialogue poetry such as the Provençal *tenson* and the Middle High German *Wechsel,* concerning which modern critics are obliged to posit separate authorship for the speeches of each participant in the dialogue in order to preserve the notion of personal poetry. Common sense and the evidence of the poetry itself tells us that little personal poetry in any sense of the word was likely to have been written during the Middle Ages, and that the concept was not readily conceivable in those cultures which were yet to invent, or were in the process of inventing, the notion of claiming authorship.

What does distinguish the medieval lyric from all other medieval literary genres is not the first-person pronoun or the identity of poet and speaker, but rather the subjectivity of the speaker: the speaker's conception of her-, him-, or itself as a *subject,* an I. William Elford Rogers, in his recent book on the lyric genre, thinks of it this way: whereas in the epic the mind of the work can only think and tell about the world of the work, in the lyric, the mind of the work "has possibilities in the world it talks about" (69). To have possibilities in the world is to be a subject, and thus someone who for others can be a You. This is how we are able innately to identify lyric poems as such: by participating in the I-You relationships they offer us. Albright writes that lyric poetry "posits a half-world or metaworld where there exists no author, no reader, no commonplace earth, only a writhe of feelings and notions, sensations attributable to no one in particular" (ix). Although Albright does not discuss the reason for the disappearance of the author and reader in lyric poems, it is easy to see why this is so. Author and reader, poet and audience, belong to the world of objective reality. In a lyric poem, which occurs only in the discourse between I and You, this objective reality momentarily, and magically, dissolves. It seems that there is only one formal restriction on lyric poetry: to be brief. And now we can see why brevity is necessary. Human beings can maintain discourse in the I–You world for only brief moments before the You reverts to an It. Discourse of any great length necessarily involves the emergence of objective reality, the establishment of a world (Albright 27).

Oral, Manuscript, and Print Cultures

The Old English lyrics have come down to us in various manuscripts, variously damaged and incomplete. The Exeter Book, written in the tenth century, comprises a wondrous collection of lyrics and riddles (many of which are discussed in these pages), as well as didactic verse, all of which is arranged in what appears to the modern reader to be a haphazard order. The Vercelli Book, also dating from the tenth century, comprises chiefly homiletic and hagiographical material in verse and prose, including "The Dream of the Rood" and the lyric epilogues of two of Cynewulf's narratives, "Fates of the Apostles" and *Elene*. The remaining lyrics are found in various prose texts dating from the eighth to the twelfth century.

Modern scholars have traditionally placed the composition of the poems much earlier than the date of the manuscripts, but this assumption has been seriously questioned in recent years, and rightly so. Norman F. Blake, for example, has made a sound case for dating the bulk of the verse in the Exeter and Vercelli Books to the Alfredian period (the late ninth through early tenth centuries), thus placing it firmly in a manuscript culture rather than in the earlier oral culture. The theory that Old English poetry was composed by unlettered singers in the oral-formulaic manner described by Albert B. Lord in *The Singer of Tales* is also no longer regarded as tenable by most scholars. In any case, lettered composition cannot be seriously contested with regard to the lyrics, since Lord's oral-formulaic theory depends solely on the evidence of long narrative poems, and is not amenable to nonnarrative verse of any kind (Stevik "Oral-Formulaic" 387).[3]

Nevertheless, although composed with pen rather than harp,[4] the Old English lyrics, like the poetry of other early manuscript cultures, are in many features closer to the poetry of an oral culture than to that of our own print culture. What follows in this section is a compendium of that information on orality, literacy, and transitional cultures which seems to me most necessary to rehearse in order to establish just how and where our notions of the Old

English lyrics differ from the notions of the people who generated them.

Walter Ong lists nine features of orally composed verbal art, seven of which are typical of the Old English lyrics (36–57).

1) Their syntax is additive rather than subordinative; that is, coordinating conjunctions vastly outnumber subordinating conjunctions. This feature is responsible for the trouble we have in determining the sequence of events in such poems as "The Wife's Lament," and in determining the relationship among parts of a poem such as "The Seafarer," which seems to us to be glued together with the troublesome adverb *forþon*.

2) Orally composed poems are aggregative rather than analytic, relying on formulas and epithets to build the poem. Epithets are not a feature of the Old English lyrics, although they appear frequently in narrative poems such as *Beowulf,* but the lyrics are certainly formulaic. Ong explains why formulaic expression is necessary in oral works: "In an oral culture, to think through something in non-formulaic, non-patterned, non-mnemonic terms, even if it were possible, would be a waste of time, for such thought, once worked through, could never be recovered with any effectiveness, as it could be with the aid of writing" (35). Works in an oral culture must be memorizable, and formulas, along with balanced syntax, sound repetition (in the case of Old English, alliteration), and thematic settings achieve memorablity (34). Eric Havelock points out that the earliest Greek works composed as texts, the poems of "Hesiod," employ language that is "basically Homeric"—that is, oral (*Muse* 79).

3) Oral works are redundant. Because the composer cannot look back on what she has just said, and the audience cannot look back on what they have just heard, repetition is necessary for coherence and comprehension.

4) The requirements of memorability result in a poetic corpus that is conservative or traditional. Because knowledge will disappear if it is not continually repeated, knowledge becomes conservative, and intellectual and artistic experimentation is inhibited. As Havelock writes, "Surprise . . . is anathema to the oral composer, because it is anathema to the oral memory" (*Literate* 141). Furthermore, in oral cultures the chief function of poetry is in fact the establishment and storage of the cultural tradition (Havelock *Muse* 71). Hence the extreme seriousness of the earliest written texts of any *ethnos*, including the bulk of Old English literature.

5) Oral poetry is situational and concrete rather than abstract. Abstract analysis is possible only in a text culture because memo-

rablity is not "friendly," to use Havelock's term, to abstract principles (*Literate* 139).

6) Furthermore, oral poetry is close to the human lifeworld. "[O]ral cultures must conceptualize and verbalize all their knowledge with more or less close reference to the human lifeworld, assimilating the alien, objective world to the more immediate, familiar interaction of human beings" (42). In oral cultures, the subjects of all statements are agents, either persons or personifications (Havelock *Muse* 76). This point is key to our understanding of the astonishing degree to which the Old English lyric poems employ personification and the pathetic fallacy. Only when a well-developed literacy obviates the need for memorability can subjects of discourse be abstract concepts rather than agents (Havelock *Muse* 101). It is therefore not surprising that Old English prose, which is a product of a lettered culture, often deals with abstractions while the contemporary verse, which has its roots in oral culture, usually does not.

7) Finally, oral poetry is empathetic and participatory rather than objectively distanced. Of course, audiences in an oral culture are physically present with the singer when a poem occurs, and this presence encourages empathy and identification. Furthermore, in an oral culture, knowing and remembering are enhanced by identification with the known. Objectivity and distance are the result of well established literacy, and are apparently not possible in an oral culture, and not probable in an early manuscript culture.

It is interesting to note here that three of the features of oral poetry listed above are also characteristic of lyric poetry originating in a print culture. Such lyric poetry does not, of course, commonly feature additive syntax, formulaic expressions, and redundancy, nor is it usually traditional. On the contrary, lyric poetry in our print culture is considered "good" when it strikes the reader as fresh, original, and innovative. However, concreteness, engagement, and the assimilation of the objective world (the I–It world) to human interaction (the I–You world) are all features of "good" lyric poetry in any culture.

At this point we need to look more closely at the early manuscript culture that produced the Old English lyric poems. Literacy in the Middle Ages had far different implications than it does in our culture. The vast majority of the population, including the nobility, was "illiterate," but this designation should have none of the pejorative connotations of ignorance that it has today. Yet medieval culture was literate in that both the Church and governments depended on written documents in order to function, and those in positions of power or responsibility needed to have access to the knowledge and information embodied in written documents (Bäuml 237), but such access did not necessarily depend on an individual's ability to read and write (Bäuml 243). Persons who could read preferred in many cases to have manuscripts read to them. M. T. Clanchy cites a description by Gerald of Wales of an audience with Pope Innocent III in 1200. The pope is shown "browsing through a reference book as a modern literate would do; but when at the subsequent audience the pope needs to absorb carefully the details of the letter, he has it read to him instead of scrutinizing it. . . . [H]e evidently found it easier to concentrate when he was listening than when he was looking; reading was still primarily oral rather than visual" (215). Clanchy also points out that the habit of sending missives was slow to develop (68). Even among persons who could read, messages were usually spoken by the messenger, and their authenticity was attested by an accompanying object (like the rune staff in "The Husband's Message") rather than by the handwriting or signature of the sender, as they are today. As for writing, it was not commonly taught as the companion of reading until about 1200 (Clanchy 102). Writing with a quill on parchment was a humble craft requiring special training that had little to do with distinctively scholarly pursuits (Clanchy 88), and thus few learned persons other than monks who wrote their own compositions out of humility (Clanchy 97) bothered to master it. Literacy in the early Middle Ages, then, was what Havelock calls "craft literacy": writing, and to a lesser extent, reading, were limited to a restricted group of persons who were employed by the learned and powerful (*Literate* 188).

Thus, early manuscript cultures remain "marginally oral" in that their manuscripts serve chiefly to recycle knowledge back into oral discourse (Ong 119). Such cultures are also marginally oral in that their manuscripts often mimic or record an oral performance or oral transaction. In the case of poetry, the work is either dictated to a scribe or, if written by the composer, dictated to oneself. As Ong writes, "You scratch out on a surface words you imagine yourself saying aloud in some realizable oral setting" (26). In the case of documents, the oral and performative act which they record is binding and complete without the written document (Stock 48). Documents are not recognized as authoritative because they serve only to remind the reader of an oral transaction, not to substitute for one. Thus, the changes wrought by writing were gradual: the introduction of literacy did not suddenly transform an oral culture into a literate one, but gradually worked to produce the kind of authority and distance we now expect from written discourse.

Writing suggests and effects distance of all kinds. In oral cultures, the poet often is present with his audience during the presentation of the poem, whether he recites it himself or employs a professional singer as the Gaelic court poets did (Finnegan 83); in print cultures, he is absent, and usually unknown to his readers. This change came about gradually in medieval England. In a manuscript culture, the poet composes in solitude (although not in silence), but he often reads his own work to his audience. As late as the fifteenth century we find Geoffrey Chaucer portrayed as doing just that. Poetry in a manuscript culture was essentially communal not only because the poet often read his own works, but because the audience for the work was more likely to be an *audience* in the original sense of the word—a *group* of auditors rather than individuals who read the work privately. The large size of early manuscript books is one indication that they were intended for reading aloud in a communal setting. In England, it was not until after 1066, with the growth of private reading, that books were made small enough to be carried in one's pocket (Clanchy 105). The tenth-century Junius, Vercelli, and Exeter Books, for example, all measure approximately twelve by eight inches—about the size of the compact edition of the *OED!*[5] It was in Norman England, not in Anglo-Saxon England, that reading came to be increasingly the solitary activity that it is today.

This gradual change in poetry from a communal to a private activity of course diminishes the possibility of dialogue among the poet and the various members of her audience. Manuscripts, however, preserve some of the capability for dialogue in ways impossible for printed books. Since early manuscripts were communally owned (by monasteries and cathedrals), any marginal notes written by one member of the community would be read by other interested persons, unlike my marginal notes, which make my books so valuable to me that I am quite reluctant to lend them. Moreover, manuscripts, although not nearly as flexible as oral discourse, are less rigid than printed books, in that scribes often incorporated marginal notes and their own additions, deletions, and "corrections" into a fresh copy of the text (Ong 132).

Although writing itself makes words seem like things rather than events (Ong 11), this process had not gone so far as it would with the introduction of moveable type and the printed word (Ong 118). Titles—labels which identify a work as a thing—were not yet necessary as they would be in the centuries to come when texts took on fixed form and came to be used as reference tools—sources of information to be looked up and used. This distance that writing gradually created between the composer and his audience produces the ability of readers to confront the text critically, as though it were a static object. What had been "a mobile relationship between linguistic sound and its recipient" becomes "[a] static relationship between the 'true' statement and its 'knower'" (Havelock *Muse* 115). The Scholastics had not yet developed the concept of objective information (as opposed to the earlier concept of individual understanding), which would come to separate the knower from the knowledge (Stock 328). And the concept of private ownership of words, which saw its full emergence in the copyright laws of the eighteenth century, was rare before the invention of the printed text (Ong 131).[6] In short, the Anglo-Saxons had not yet hypostatized discourse.

Poet and Audience

Many questions involving the relationship among poem, poet, and audience have already raised themselves in the discussion above, and now we can address them more specifically. The notion of authorship is linked to the hypostatization of the poem. In a print culture, a poem is the property of the historical individual who created it: the author. We are all familiar with the attempts of the New Critics to discount the role of the author, and many of us have experimented in our classrooms with offering students a poem for analysis with the name of the author excised, but whether or not the name is known, we, and our students, clearly understand that the poem was in fact composed by someone, and if we want to quote from it, we had better find out her name or we commit plagiarism.

Our culture acknowledges the prestige of the individual, and so it is natural for us to believe that knowledge of the author and his life and times will explain his work. After all, it matters a great deal when we read "When I Have Fears" that Keats was dying of tuberculosis, or, to take an example from a late manuscript culture, when we read "To Rosemounde" that its author was the plump, hard-working civil servant Geoffrey Chaucer—satire is possible only in a culture that acknowledges authorship. But when we come to Old English poetry, such questions become irrelevant. We say that Old English poetry is anonymous, but the word is deceiving. To say that a letter to the editor or a ransom note is anonymous means that the author's name has been purposely suppressed. To say that a poem is anonymous means that the author's name has been lost—unfortunately. But to say that the Old English poems are anonymous is to say that they are not only unsigned, but that they originate from a culture that had little concept of property rights over works of verbal art. Therefore, to ask whether Shakespeare wrote this or that anonymous poem and whether Caedmon wrote this or that anonymous poem is to ask two very different questions: the second question is nugatory, since Caedmon himself seems to have disavowed responsibility for composing his poems. According to Bede, Caedmon, an illiterate cowherd at the monastery of Whitby in the late seventh century, generated his first poem this way:

> Suddenly in a dream he saw a man standing beside him who called him by name. "Caedmon," he said, "sing me a song." "I don't know how to sing," he replied. "It is because I cannot sing that I left the feast and came here." The man who addressed him then said: "But you shall sing to me." "What should I sing about?" he replied. "Sing about the Creation of all things," the other answered. And Caedmon immediately began to sing verses in praise of God the Creator that he had never heard before. . . . When Caedmon awoke, he remembered everything that he had sung in his dream, and soon added more verses in the same style to a song truly worthy of God. (Bk. 4, ch. 24)

Bede's interpretation of this event, which must have occurred when he was about seven years old, is that Caedmon "did not acquire the art of poetry from men or through any human teacher but received it as a free gift from God" (Bk. 4, ch. 24).

Caedmon was an illiterate oral poet who apparently did not sign any of his poems: probably none of his work (other than the nine lines associated with Bede's story) has survived. However, we find this same notion of composing in a later, signed, lettered composition: Cynewulf's *Elene:*

Ic wæs weorcum fah,
synnum asæled,   sorgum gewæled,
bitrum gebunden,   bisgum beþrungen,
ær me lare onlag   þurh leohtne had
gamelum to geoce,   gife unscynde
mægencyning amæt   ond on gemynd begeat,
torht ontynde,   tidum gerymde,
bancofan onband,   brestlocan onwand,
leoðucræft onleac.

(1242b–50a)

[I was stained with my (evil) deeds, fettered with sins, raging with sorrows, bitterly bound, pressed by troubles, before the King of Might gave me learning by means of light, bestowed and infused in my mind a glorious gift as a help for my old age, and revealed clearness, at times opened up, unbound my body, unwound my heart, unlocked the art of song.]

Cynewulf is the only Anglo-Saxon poet in the vernacular to sign his name to his works, and the fact that he, too, credits God for his talent demonstrates a deeply held notion of the relative inconsequence of the individual artist.

For the Anglo-Saxons, the composition of oral poetry, which surely persisted among the unlettered throughout the Anglo-Saxon period, seems to have been an ordinary and democratic endeavor. Caedmon left his fellows at a beer-drinking party because he was the only one in attendance who could not sing, while at the other end of the social spectrum, the *Beowulf* poet shows a Danish warrior composing extemporaneously at a horse race. For us, however, it is difficult to imagine the production of works of art without idolatry of the artist. Imagine having a friend recommend attending a concert because, "A pianist is going to play a sonata." Our response would be, "What pianist? And whose sonata?" The composition and execution of piano sonatas are beyond most people's abilities nowadays, so it is natural that the artist is esteemed above ordinary people. Of course, we do practice some democratic art forms: folk art such as tole painting or quilting has gone unsigned until recently, clearly because the tole painter and quilter, like the medieval poet, are working in a tradition and have not see themselves as innovators or creators, but merely as the person who happened to execute this particular piece. Some new forms such as Xerox art, mail art, clip art, and the like are inherently democratic because they do not require special training: anyone, with a little practice, can put together a successful piece of Xerox art, and many of the people who practice such art forms do so consciously rejecting the concept of the artist as a special person. Interestingly, these forms are conventionally not signed, unless by a cognomen that sounds something like a "CB handle"—a kind of reverse snobbery. But fewer and fewer forms of art circulate without the creator's name attached. Even story-telling has fallen into the hands of specialists—folksy specialists, to be sure, but story-telling is no longer something every grandmother can and does do.

While oral composition was apparently a democratic endeavor among the Anglo-Saxons, written composition was surely narrowly restricted to the monastic elite, whether they wrote their own compositions or dictated them to others.[7] Clinton Albertson writes that it was a common practice for the upper classes to enter monastic life in middle age, pointing to Cuthbert, who is thought to have served in Oswy's army, and Benedict Biscop, who was a member of Oswy's personal retainers (10). Asser's *Life of Alfred* tells us that John the Old Saxon, a monk whom Alfred brought to Wessex to help him restore learning in England, was "a man with some experience in the martial arts" (ch. 97). Albertson estimates that some thirty Anglo-Saxon kings and their wives left their thrones to become monks and nuns between 613 and 829: "the number of royal abbesses is astounding" (19). Thus, it was not only noble monks who became scribes, scholars, and writers, but noble nuns as well. As Dorothy Whitelock points out, "Aldhelm's writings for the nuns of Barking and Rudolf's *Life of St. Leofgyth . . .* show that women, like men, studied the scriptures and their fourfold interpretation, the works of the Fathers, chronology, grammar, and metrics" (*Beginnings* 198).

Most of the women writers whose names have come down to us (like most of the men) seem to have written only in Latin—nuns such as Hrotswith, who wrote Latin verse legends, and Hygeburh, who wrote the Latin *Lives of St. Willibald and St. Wynnebald*—but there is occasional mention of nuns writing in the vernacular, such as Alcuin's prohibition against nuns writing love songs. That this phenomenon is more often ignored by modern scholars than not may be seen in this typical statement on known writers of the period: "Apart from the casual mention of nuns with poetic gifts, we have only three names with which we may connect the 30,000 or more surviving lines of Anglo-Saxon verse: Caedmon, Aldhelm, and Cynewulf."[8] Oddly enough, while this statement clearly intends to emphasize male authorship, it backhandedly implies that all but three of the known Anglo-Saxon poets were women, a circumstance well worth noting if it is true. Of course, I would not want to argue for a woman author of any particular piece, but we should keep in mind that the authors of these lyrics were likely both men and women of good education who had a religious vocation *and* some secular experience.

Nevertheless, the Anglo-Saxons obviously did not attach any extraordinary prestige to the act of verbal composition, and it is not because they did not value individual action. Genealogies were important, as were the names of heroes. Also, other artwork, such as jewelry, swords, or memorial stones, was occasionally signed. And so were prose treatises. As Foucault points out:

> Even within our civilization, the same types of texts have not always required authors; there was a time when those texts which we now call "literary" (stories, folktales, epics, and tragedies) were accepted, circulated, and valorized without any question about the identity of their author. Their anonymity was ignored because their real or supposed age was a sufficient guarantee of their authenticity. Texts, however, that we now call "scientific" (dealing with cosmology and the heavens, medicine or illness, the natural sciences or geography) were only considered truthful during the Middle Ages if the name of the author was indicated. . . . In the seventeenth and eighteenth centuries, a totally new conception was developed when scientific texts were accepted on their own merits and positioned within an anonymous and coherent conceptual system of established truths and methods of verification. Authentification no longer required reference to the individual who had produced them. . . . At the same time, however, "literary" discourse was acceptable only if it carried an author's name. (125–26)

Perhaps the biggest barrier to our ability to read Old English poetry is the odd concept of the lyric as a form of self-expression. We have already seen, for example, that Jakobson pairs the emotive mode of lyric poetry with the use of the first person, and, although we are post-Romantics, or think we are, the fact that much of the great lyric poetry in English was composed during the Romantic era prejudices our thinking about the lyric poet as somehow synonymous with the lyric speaker. An irony of this Romantic concept, or our understanding of it, is that John Keats himself maintained that the poet has no identity. In a letter to Richard Woodhouse (27 October 1818), Keats discusses the concept he elsewhere had called Negative Capability: the obliteration of the poet's ego in his identification with and absorption in another being.

> A Poet is the most unpoetical of any thing in existence; because he has no Identity—he is continually in for—and filling some other Body— The Sun, the Moon, the Sea and Men and Women who are creatures of impulse are poetical and have about them an unchangeable attribute— the poet has none; no identity. . . . It is a wretched thing to confess; but it is a very fact that not one word I ever utter can be taken for granted as an opinion growing out of my identical nature—how can it, when I have no nature? When I am in a room with People if I ever am free from speculating on creations of my own brain, then not myself goes home to myself: but the identity of every one in the room begins to press upon me that, I am in a very little time anhilated [sic]—not only among Men; it would be the same in a Nursery of children. (1220)

Indeed, for Keats, it was the same in the company of sparrows: "if a Sparrow come before my Window I take part in its existence and pick about the Gravel" (Letter to Benjamin Baily, 22 November 1817, p. 1208). In the case of anonymous, conventional texts, like the Old English lyrics, the "I" of the poem, if there is an "I," is even less likely to refer to the "extra-linguistic" reality of the author, for manuscript cultures only gradually discover the concept of selfhood by means of the gradual separation of the knower from the known that literacy fosters (Havelock *Muse* 5).[9]

Modern audiences for poetry, and *belles lettres* of any kind, are quite different from the Anglo-Saxon audience for works of verbal art. Poets today write for an elite audience which consists chiefly of scholars and other poets: my neighbors, parents, and lower-division students do not read poetry or attend readings. For those of us who do, poetry is serious business, an enrichment activity that we take like vitamin E. One does not drink beer or eat pretzels or flirt with a fellow member of the audience at a poetry reading, although we commonly do such things when we engage in a "popular culture" activity, such as watching a videotape. For us, poetry usually means reading, and reading is inappropriate in a group setting: most of us who ended up as English teachers can remember being admonished by our parents not to read at the breakfast table. For the Anglo-Saxons, however, the presentation of poetry often accompanied the communal and convivial activities of eating and drinking, and this was probably true even of clerics, as the stain of a beer mug on a page of the Exeter Book indicates. The differences between the modern audience and the Anglo-Saxon audience are even more dramatic in the case of Old English poetry, which has gone, as Socrates feared in the *Phaedrus*, where it was not intended to go (275e). The modern audience for Old English poems, other than *Beowulf,* which is frequently read in translation by undergraduate students, is composed almost exclusively of scholars: erudite specialists in the Old English language or, perhaps, literature. To state the perfectly obvious, Old English poetry was not intended for such an audience. Benjamin contrasts audiences that concentrate on the work with those that are distracted (241). Clearly, we concentrate very hard on poetry that was composed for a distracted audience.

Aside from the makeup of the audience and the manner of presentation, further differences have to do with culturally conditioned expectations of what constitutes a good work of verbal art. As teachers of composition never tire of saying, our chief criteria are unity and coherence. In "Literature and Discontinuity," Barthes writes that we tolerate discontinuity only when the work is fragmentary, or unfinished, or when it is explicitly a collection of aphorisms (174). However, in the case of fragmentary or unfinished works, we assume continuity and coherence in the original or in the plan—we will never have done with trying to put *The Canterbury Tales* in order. Even if we deny the necessity of unity, we still use this notion in our reading, and even more so in our editing practices. We choose explanations that relate parts of a poem rather than those that separate parts. Confronted with a fragment, we fill gaps on the assumption of unity. For us, "unity" usually means binary opposition and its resolution, but modern concepts of what constitutes unity are not those of the Middle Ages. As D. W. Robertson illustrates so well, our penchant for opposition and synthesis is a modern convention, while medieval concepts of unity were based rather on symmetrical and hierarchical patterning (6 and passim.) Robertson, of course, is speaking of the High Middle Ages, and it is not at all clear whether one ought to apply his medieval definition of unity to Old English literature, but nevertheless, the realization that the concept of a unified, coherent work of art varies according to culture should caution us about our interpretive and editorial practices. The Old English poems for the most part exist in unique manuscripts, many of which are missing pages or have been damaged in spots. Even when we can be fairly sure that we have a complete text, the manuscript often does not clearly indicate where one poem ends and another begins, since all the works are untitled. In reading and editing the poems, therefore, we tend to fill gaps and to divide lines of verse into discrete works based upon our own assumptions of unity and coherence, which quite clearly were not those of the Anglo-Saxons.

Given the obvious fact that we are not a very appropriate audience for Old English poetry, how is it that the poems can occur when we read them? Perhaps the question should be, *Are* the poems actually occurring when we read them, or are we somehow deceived by wishful thinking into believing that they are? Recent critical theory on the role of the reader tells us that our intuition is right: the poetry *is* occurring. "Skilled reading," Stanley Fish writes, is an activity not of discerning, but rather of producing, not of construing, but of constructing, not of decoding, but of making (327). The text is no more freestanding than the reader, and it occurs only when it is read. Language, the stuff of verbal art, is a social phenomenon, and any linguistic event must therefore take place in some milieu. Regardless of the fact that we are not the author's intended readers, we are actual readers nevertheless, and neither more nor less handicapped by our cultural background than any other actual reader, even the intended reader, who is restricted in time and space just as much as we. This is how works of art differ from objects that have no other being than their thingliness. An Anglo-Saxon spinning whorl is an object made for the use of a group of people that does not include me. It exists now, but its use is limited to a culture in which I do not participate, and it continues to exist whether or not it is used. A poem, however, requires an audience—and not just the intended audience—in order to occur. Without *me,* the poem exists only as an object, black ink in a green book.

The reading of any lyric poem is an ontological inquiry. The lyric poem represents an emotion, and the reader recollects it, or re-experiences it, or re-views it. But that emotion is not merely re-experienced, for the lyric poem forces us to re-view the emotion through the eyes of another, the speaker of the poem. The emotion is achieved by means of another consciousness, and thus occurs the breakdown of the ontological barriers between "I" and "Other" into a relationship of "I" and "You." The reader and the speaker face each other as two human beings. Reading a lyric poem illuminates Being by removing taxonomic walls that have been built in our attempts to achieve selfhood—to define ourselves as "I" by positing all else as "Other." Readers of a radically anonymous poem have the advantage over readers of a signed poem, because, for the latter, the knowledge and acknowledgement of an author interferes with the direct interaction between reader and speaker. In other words, the presence of an author (in the mind of the reader if not in the text of the poem) erects another ontological barrier. When I read "When I Have Fears," for example, I begin to feel the emotion of the speaker of the poem, but I find half of myself resisting engagement with him because, Negative Capability notwithstanding, I know for sure that a historical person, John Keats, wrote this poem when he was dying of consumption, and I am not John Keats and do not share his ill health. So with lyric poetry, the absence of an author is a help rather than a hindrance to reading, for it encourages more immediate identification of the reader with the speaker.

The Lyric Speaker

Now we see why the lyric speaker is central to the successful occurrence of a lyric poem. Jakobson, in his classification of the types of verbal communication, and Benveniste, in his study of the concept of person in grammar, each provides us with the suggestion that discourse (such as epic poetry) that refers to a context external to the relationship between the discoursers is substantially different from discourse (such as lyric poetry) that derives its meaning from the discourse itself. Buber's distinction of the I-You relationship from the I-It relationship further sharpens the dichotomy by describing the I-You relationship as an evanescent and even uncanny realization of an Other as a subject in her own right. Buber's description of the fleeting I-You encounter, which can occasionally punctuate our ordinary lives of I-It relationships, is strikingly similar to the occurrence of a lyric poem.

Thus far we find that lyric poetry is consistently associated not only with the recognition of subjectivity and with relationships between subjects—all of which implies the primary importance of the speaker—but also with the actual occurrence off first- and second-person pronouns in the discourse. Since most of the lyric poetry with which most of us are familiar does indeed employ first- and second-person pronouns, I began this study fascinated but perplexed that many of the Old English poems that felt like lyrics lacked an I (all of them lack a You), and most of the others employed an I who was pretty hard to identify with an Anglo-Saxon poet of *any* stereotype—unlettered singer or monkish scribe. This situation seemed a crux to me then: although it gave the poems a feel of otherness, strangeness, it yet proved no obstacle to reading and engaging with them as one would read and engage with lyric poems of more familiar eras which depend so heavily on the personal I. How can the lack of the first- and second-person pronouns be accounted for when their presence seems to the theorists to be essential—to be of the essence of the lyric? William Elford Rogers, in *The Three Genres and the Interpretation of the Lyric,* answers the question. Discussing the lyrics that the theorists ignore, Rogers designates those without an I as "impersonal" lyrics and those with an I who "cannot possibly be the author" (78) as "anomalous voice" lyrics. In the impersonal lyrics, he writes, the mind of the work not only reproduces a world (which is what the mind of the epic does) but also finds itself in the work it reproduces (104). The impersonal lyric in fact catches the I at the moment it becomes aware of itself (106). This assertion puts the impersonal lyric well within Rogers's definition of the lyric quoted above: a poem in which the mind of the work "has possibilities in the world it talks about" (69). As for the anomalous voice, Rogers suggests that it is not merely a mouthpiece for the poet (82), but rather a way in which the poet can encounter himself through empathy with another (84–85). The anomalous voice poems likewise provide the reader with an opportunity—or better, a mandate—to empathize with the speaker, and the reader of such poems thus finds it impossible to remain detached (88).

Rogers's categories make a great deal of sense to me because they do what Frye argued concerning genre criticism: they bring "out a large number of literary relationships that would not be noticed as long as there were no context established for them." In addition, they demonstrate that poems without an I and poems in which the I cannot be identified with the author both provide special opportunities for the reader (and poet) and are thus not at all marginal members of the larger lyric genre. Our glance back into the early manuscript culture that generated the Old English lyric has provided many further suggestions as to why the Anglo-Saxons may have eschewed personal speakers in their lyric poetry in favor of other kinds of speakers. The marginal orality of written documents meant that they were not a substitute for oral events but rather merely an aid in remembering such events or in regenerating them. Written discourse was not yet hypostatized because it was constantly being recycled into oral events. The Anglo-Saxons were unaware of our concepts both of the authorship of poetry, which is linked to its hypostatization, and of self-expression, which is possible only after the concept of the individual has taken root in a culture. Various persons reading aloud to "live" audiences poems composed by various (and unknown) persons in various voices is hardly an environment conducive to the generation of our concept of personal poetry.

Given, then, that opening lines like "That time of year that thou mayst in me behold," let alone "Shall I compare thee to a summer's day?" are scarcely to be expected, what choices did an Anglo-Saxon singer or scribe have from which to choose a speaker for his lyric poem? Of course, the notion of choosing a speaker would doubtless have been incomprehensible to the Anglo-Saxons, but nevertheless their lyrics do employ a wide variety of speakers from an onion to a poet with just about every stop in between. What topics, moods, or occasions demanded or suggested a particular type of speaker? What topics, moods, or occasions suggested a speaker who never identifies himself at all? Can certain kinds of speakers be identified with a particular time, place, or style? How does the choice (or requirement) of a certain kind of speaker limit or enhance a poet's possibilities in a lyric? It was questions like these that prompted my own decision to examine the Old English lyrics by grouping them according to their speakers.

What follows is my own taxonomy of Old English lyric speakers, arranged in what I take to be roughly the chronological order of the development of the type (*not* the chronological order of the poems themselves), beginning with the certainly primeval inanimate speaker and moving ahead to the certainly modern personal speaker. Rogers's impersonal speaker appears here as the nonpersonal speaker, since I find that the word "impersonal" carries inappropriate connotations of emotionlessness. His anomalous voice is here as the fictive and inanimate speakers. I've added one more category for the prayers and charms, the adoptable speaker, and I end with a chapter on the speakers of the two masterpieces of the Anglo-Saxon lyric: "The Dream of the Rood" and "The Wanderer." I have no doubt that the Old English lyrics, whose very essence is the rupture of taxonomies, can survive my meddling.

Part II
The Poems

2
The Inanimate Speaker

The term "inanimate speaker" is clearly a paradox. The Anglo-Saxon poets often used the expression *reordberend* "speech-bearer" for "human being," demonstrating that they, like we, posited speech to be the distinguishing feature of our kind. All speakers are therefore by definition not only animate, but human. But the paradox implicit in the term "inanimate speaker" mirrors the paradox implicit in the lyrics that employ such a speaker. In chapter 1 we saw that lyric poetry breaks through ontological taxonomies. In this chapter, we will see how the inanimate speaker breaks down the distinctions between human and nonhuman, animate and inanimate, natural and social.

Lyrics, other than the riddles, that use inanimate speakers are few in number, but the tradition from which they sprang was surely an ancient one. Eric Havelock, discussing the beginnings of Greek literacy, believes it likely that the Greek alphabet was invented for use in dedicatory inscriptions (*Muse* 85), which were frequently in the first-person voice of the object inscribed: for example, "I am Nestor's cup" or "Mantiklos dedicated me" (*Literate* 191). Such inscriptions were common in Greece before 400 B.C.E. but rare after that date. Havelock's explanation is that in cultures that do not employ written documentation of transactions, inscriptions are made in the voice of the object inscribed because the object, unlike the persons involved in the transaction, is permanent. Once documentation is widely employed, prosopopoeic inscriptions are no longer necessary, since the written document provides the desired permanence of the transaction (*Literate* 191, 206 n.9).

Archeological evidence from the Germanic Dark Ages appears to support Havelock's theory. Prosopopoeic inscriptions in the runic alphabet antedate the introduction of the Roman alphabet. Albert S. Cook observes that "epigrams in the first person are to be found in every literary period since at least the fifth century. . . . They were cast on bells . . . , carved or painted on the front of houses and chapels in Germany and Switzerland, and engraved on swords"

(*Dream* xliv–xlv). There are many extant examples of prosopopoeic epigrams in Old English, among them the ninth-century Alfred jewel, inscribed, "Ælfred mec heht gewyrcean" [Alfred had me made]; the Gospel manuscript Cotton Otho C.i, which proclaims "Wulfwi me wrat" [Wulfwi wrote me]; and the Brussels reliquary, inscribed, "Drahmal me worhte" [Drahmal made me]. Prosopopoeia appears to be stronger in cultures and languages in which literacy is a recent introduction than in those with a firm literate tradition. The Anglo-Saxon poets who wrote riddles in the vernacular made use of inanimate speakers more frequently than did Anglo-Saxons who wrote Latin riddles (Cook, *Dream* xlvii), and furthermore, "the English poets [of the riddles], even when writing in Latin, show a tendency to greater elaboration of detail and vividness of presentation, along with completer personification" (xlix).

In this chapter, I examine first four prosopopoeic manuscript prefaces, and then several Exeter Book riddles and "The Husband's Message." The prefaces have little aesthetic value, but they interest me for a couple of reasons, one of which is that they demonstrate the notion that books talk to their readers. Their speakers are either the manuscript itself, that is, Heidegger's "thingly aspect" of the work, or the work itself, that is, its "work-aspect," the literary event which is physically manifested in the manuscript. As for why the author chose the inanimate speaker for these prefaces, one can point to the reluctance in the Anglo-Saxon tradition to use the personal speaker, which is discussed more fully in chapter 6. More importantly, however, for the Anglo-Saxons a piece of writing was thought of as speaking. As the discussion of manuscript cultures in chapter 1 shows, composers in early manuscript cultures usually dictated their compositions to a scribe, or spoke aloud the words that they wrote for themselves. Audiences likewise usually received the text orally in a communal setting, or, if reading the text alone, spoke the words aloud to themselves. Furthermore, communally owned manuscripts preserve the possibility of dialogue between the author and various readers by the incorporation of marginal comments or changes in fresh copies of the text. Thus, for early manuscript cultures, books do dialogue with their readers in a very real sense. Even early charters, which mark the shift of a culture to dependence on the authority of the written word, "quite often conclude with 'Goodbye' *(Valete),* as if the donor had just finished speaking with his audience" (Clanchy 202).

The other reason that I discuss the verse prefaces in some detail is that they establish valuable precedents for the treatment that more literary inanimate speakers, such as the Cross in "The Dream of the Rood" and the speaker of "The Husband's Message," receive at the hands of their authors. Especially interesting to me in each of the manuscript prefaces is the degree of interaction (if any) between the speaker and the supposed author, and between the speaker and the intended reader.

The verse preface "Thureth" is found in Cotton Claudius A.iii, a miscellaneous volume that seems to have some of its parts displaced. The poem is probably connected with the eleventh-century coronation liturgy found in that manuscript. The speaker—identified in the first line: "Ic eom halgungboc" [I am a consecration book]—is the manuscript, and the purpose of the lyric is clearly to praise one Thureth, who commissioned the book (lines 2–3) and donated a plot of land to the church (8–9). The relationship of the manuscript-speaker to Thureth posits the personification of the manuscript: "healde hine dryhten" [I hold him lord, 1b]. The author of the poem is probably not to be understood as Thureth himself, since Thureth was not a cleric, but rather as the scribe of the *halgungboc,* who found this way of indirectly, though fulsomely, praising his benefactor. The manuscript is itself the memorial to Thureth's generosity and piety, and the poem, in personifying the manuscript, merely reiterates what the manuscript implicitly proclaims. In this, "Thureth" greatly resembles dedicatory inscriptions.

"The Metrical Preface to Waerferth's Translation of Gregory's Dialogues" appears in only one manuscript of the Old English *Dialogues.* The speaker indirectly identifies itself in the first line, "[.]e ðe me rædan ðance" [He who wishes to read me], and it proceeds to instruct the reader in its purpose, its history, and the virtues of the bishop who ordered it, ending with a request for the reader's prayers for this bishop and for his king, Alfred.[1] The author of the preface is probably the bishop, for, as Kenneth Sisam (*Studies* 225) points out, no one else would have called him "þeow and þearfa" [servant and pauper, 13a]. One further point about this "Preface": it is the only one of the four in which any great notice is taken of the reader. The first 11 lines have to do entirely with the benefits of this book for the reader, and in line 17, the book identifies itself as that "þe þu on þinum handum nu hafast and sceawast" [which you now have in your hands and examine]. Like "Thureth," this preface effectively matches its purpose to the purpose of the larger work: in "Thureth," the shared purpose of preface and book is to testify to a man's generosity, and in this poem, it is to edify the reader.

The remaining two prefaces are somewhat different in that their speakers are to be understood as the works themselves rather than the manuscripts. "The Metrical Preface to the Pastoral Care" begins in the third person with the history of Gregory's work: "Þis ærendgewrit Agustinus ofer sealtne sæ suðan brohte" [Augustine brought this writing over the salt sea from the south, 1–2]. When the speaker finally makes its appearance in the first person, it further identifies itself as Gregory's work rather than as the manuscript: "Siððan min on englisc Ælfred kyning awende worda gehwelc" [Afterwards, King Alfred translated each one of my words into English, 11–12a]. From this point through the end of the poem, the speaker tells us how Alfred disseminated his translation and for whom—"ða ðe lædenspræce læste cuðon" [those who are least competent in the Latin language, 16]. The primary business of this lyric is not praise of Gregory (although there is some of that), nor praise of Alfred (of which there is none), nor encouragement to the reader (who is only mentioned as "those who"), but rather merely to provide the history of the work. This "Preface" appears in three manuscripts, one of which is incontestably of the ninth century, and it therefore in all probability represents an original preface to the translation, perhaps even by Alfred's own hand, which would account for its modest treatment of the translation's royal patron.

The one remaining prosopopoeic preface is "Aldhelm," a mere fragment, but one of only two examples of macaronic verse in Old English (the other being the final eleven lines of "The Phoenix"). "Aldhelm" comprises three languages—Old English, Latin, and transliterated Greek—randomly arranged, and it occurs uniquely in a tenth-century manuscript of Aldhelm's *De virginitate*. The *ASPR* dismisses the poem as "simply . . . an exercise in metrical and linguistic ingenuity" (6, xcii), but the macaronic verse, although bumpy and confusing (and to a modern reader, funny), must have indicated to its intended audience an ambitious and learned speaker, which is just what a work of Aldhelm's would be if only it could speak. The speaker introduces itself in the first line as Aldhelm's treatise—"Þus me gesette" [Thus (Aldhelm) wrote me]—and reappears to describe itself: "Biblos ic nu sceal, ponus et pondus pleno cum sensu . . . secgan soð, nalles leas" [A book, a work and a weight, filled with meaning, I shall now speak the truth, nothing less, 5b–8a]. The rest of the poem as we have it is given over to praising Aldhelm. Again, we see how well this lyric fits the Anglo-Saxons' conception of Aldhelm as learned and multilingual. The speaker takes no notice of the reader, but concerns itself solely with its importance and with that of the author of the treatise. We can imagine the poem's author to have been a scribe who greatly admired Aldhelm, and who took this opportunity to express his admiration through the treatise as speaker, since he would not have been important enough in his own eyes to have spoken *in propria persona.*

Turning now to the riddles, we find not only a far greater range of speakers, but also far greater aesthetic value. There are ninety-some Exeter Book riddles, the exact number depending upon the reader's determination of whether certain continguous passages are one or two riddles, and whether the 17 lines following Riddle 30b are Riddle 60 or the beginning of "The Husband's Message," as I take them to be. These riddles take as their subjects natural phenomena, animals, agricultural and domestic tools, food and drink, weapons, books and writing paraphernalia, objects associated with Christian worship, musical instruments, genitalia, and more. Since the solutions are not given in the manuscript, for the most part, many are conjectural and some of the riddles yet lack a consensus solution.

Because riddles demand solutions from their readers, they demonstrate most clearly the kind of dialogue that all lyric poetry requires between speaker and reader. Yet, the Old English riddles, for the most part, are not difficult to solve. Many solutions are obvious despite the riddles' great age and their references to a culture in which we do not participate. Others that are problematic for us were likely obvious to the Anglo-Saxons. Some, indeed, such as Riddle 47 (Book-moth) and Riddle 23 (Bow), provide their solutions in their texts. Apparently, for the Anglo-Saxons, as for us, the joy of riddles lies in knowing the solution beforehand or in readily perceiving obvious clues.[2]

A related question is whether a good riddle allows of only one correct solution. Again, I think not. Many of the Exeter Book riddles are satisfactorily solved in several ways, especially the bird and animal riddles. In addition, all of the riddles whose solutions relate to sexual matters can be solved by common household objects, such as Riddle 44, which may be Key rather than Penis, and Riddle 77, which may be Churning Butter rather than Sexual Intercourse. If we are to read and enjoy the Exeter Book riddles, we should be free to create solutions that please us, even though we are sure that our solutions are not the intended ones. Riddle 66 is a case in point.

> Ic eom mare   þonne þes middangeard,
>   læsse þonne hondwyrm,   leohtre þonne mona,

swiftre þonne sunne.   Sæs me sind ealle
flodas on fæðmum   ond þes foldan bearm,
grene wongas.   Grundum ic hrine,
helle underhnige,   heofonas oferstige,
wuldres eþel,   wide ræce
ofer engla eard,   eorþan gefylle,
ealne middangeard   one merestreamas
side mid me sylfum.   Saga hwæt ic hatte.

[I am larger than the earth, smaller than the handworm, brighter than
the moon, swifter than the sun. The seas and all the waters, and the
earth's bosom, the green fields, are in my embrace. I lay hold of the
ground, sink under hell, climb over the heavens, the homeland of glory,
stretch out widely over the angels' land. I fill the earth, the whole world
and the ocean streams, with myself. Say what I am called.]

The solution Creation is obvious to all modern editors, and there
can be little doubt but that Creation was the solution intended by
the poet. However, this riddle interests *me* chiefly because I can
solve it pantheistically: God. My twelve-year-old daughter, who
loves this riddle as much as I do, solves it yet another way: Imagination. I know that neither God nor Imagination could have been
possible solutions for the Anglo-Saxons, but if we limit our responses to those that we know were intended, we miss the opportunity to engage the riddlic speakers and to dialogue with them. And
if we miss that opportunity, the riddles remain lifeless objects which
we can neither enjoy nor learn from. The riddle bids us, "Saga
hwæt ic hatte," and we can do no less than to answer for ourselves.

At this point I need to limit the discussion to the first-person
riddles, which make up about half of the Exeter Book collection.
The entire corpus deserves, and has been given, fuller and more
competent treatment than I am capable of giving it.[3] My purpose
here is to discuss just a few selections as illustrations of the inanimate lyric speaker. From here on, when I refer to the riddles, I
mean the first-person riddles only.

To read these riddles is to realize that they need no defense as
lyric poems.[4] We have already seen that the riddle, like the lyric
poem, demands dialogue between speaker and reader. Moreover,
its solution is achieved through the reader's identification with the
speaker. Craig Williamson compares, for example, Riddles 16 (An-
chor) and 88 (Inkhorn) with Latin riddles by Symphosius and
Eusebius.[5] In the Latin riddles, the speaker "is always a creature
outside, an *other* manipulated by the poet. The Anglo-Saxon
[speaker] is simply one of us. When we discover his plight, we

discover ourselves" (11). Like other lyric poems, and like metaphors, the riddles cut through our ontological taxonomies. By personifying the inanimate or nonhuman, they give us new insight into our world and transform the uncanny into the recognizable (Williamson 33–34).

Riddle 5 (Shield) provides a simple example of how personification leads to identification with the speaker and hence to the solution. As I summarize the riddle, I intersperse what I believe are typical responses that lead to the solution. The speaker begins by stating that he is solitary, wounded in battle, and weary of war. (Perhaps he is a captive or a thane whose lord has been killed in battle?) He has no hope for release from fighting before he perishes in fire. (Why fire?) Finally, he says that no physician can heal his wounds, which are ever increasing. (Then he cannot be human, for humans either heal or die. What is continuously wounded in battle? Armor. What piece of armor cannot be repaired and fears fire? Something made of wood: a shield.) I do not ordinarily have any sympathy for shields, but I do sympathize with this one. Initially (mis-?)taking him for human, I empathized with his weariness of war and his wounded condition. By the time I discovered that he is only a shield, it was too late to recant: I had shared his self-pity as being worse off than a human warrior.

Riddle 88 (Inkhorn) works in a similar fashion. The first nine lines are illegible, but thereafter we have a speaker telling us that he and his brother once dwelt together under the sheltering forest, but they have since been replaced by two younger brothers. The speaker now stands immobile on a table. He does not know the whereabouts of his brother, but remembers the time when they battled together. Now a monster has hollowed him out. He cannot return. The answer is obviously a horn, more specifically an inkhorn, since drinking horns do not stand in fixed positions. The necessary clue to this solution lies in the speaker's focus on his brother, a metaphor that indicates that the speaker is an object that occurs, in its natural state, in pairs. Without this emphasis on his brother, the other clues could indicate any vessel carved from stone, bone, or wood. Brotherhood is therefore the focus of the speaker's monologue, and it is also the focus of the reader's emotional response. We empathize with his exile from his home and, even more, with his separation from his brother and companion. It is quite clear from the beginning of the text as we have it that the speaker cannot be human, but nevertheless, he succeeds in gaining our empathy by speaking to us in the terms of the human lifeworld: permanent separation from a beloved brother.

I want to take one more example of a riddle that uses personification to encourage our empathy, but this one carries the personification to a bizarre extreme and more strongly focuses our thoughts
away from the speaker and onto our own experiences. The speaker
of Riddle 20 (Sword) begins by giving himself away. (I find it very
difficult to refer to these speakers as "it," as I did in the four
prefaces, which tells me just how successful these riddles are in
gaining my empathy.) In the first two lines, he says that he is a
wonderful thing, made for battle, dear to his lord, and beautifully
adorned. The reader thus knows from the beginning that he must be
some weapon or article of armor, and is most likely a sword, since
the Anglo-Saxon warrior especially valued his sword—indeed, the
literature gives us many swords with names. But from here on, the
reader is in for a great deal of confusion. The third line refers to the
speaker's byrnie: since swords do not wear mailshirts, we are ready
to retract our initial assumption until it becomes obvious that the
byrnie is a metaphor for the decoration on the sword's hilt, and that
this metaphor personifies the sword. He then says that he kills men
with "battleweapons," which is wholly inexplicable to readers still
identifying the speaker as a sword, throwing us back again to
thinking of him as a human warrior. The speaker goes on to describe how his lord praises and honors him in the meadhall, which
makes sense for either a man or a sword, but although he is honored
by his lord, he is also outlawed and denounced, a paradox that
likewise makes sense for both a man and sword, for what the victor
praises, the victim curses. From here on, the speaker describes
ways in which he differs from human thanes: he will leave no child
to avenge him or to increase his tribe, and must forfeit the pro-
creative act. The end of the riddle is lost, but the last lines that we
have read thus:

                Ic wiþ bryde ne mot
hæmed habban,   ac me þæs hyhtplegan
geno wyrneð,   se mec geara on
bende legde;   forþon ic brucan sceal
on hagostealde   hæleþa gestreona.
Oft ic wirum dol   wife abelge,
wonie hyre willan;   heo me wom speceð,
floceð hyre folmum,   firenaþ mec wordum,
ungod gæleð.   Ic ne gyme þæs compes

(27b-35)

[I am not able to cohabit with a bride, for he who of yore laid me in bonds (i.e., his owner) denies me this joyous play. Therefore I must enjoy the treasures of heroes in a state of celibacy. Often, foolish with wire ornaments, I anger a woman, diminish her desires. She howls at me, claps her hands, curses me with words, screams evil. I take no notice of this struggle's . . .]

How does the riddle arrive at this gruesome scene? The sword has been speaking of himself in human terms, evoking no particular emotional response from the reader, and then he chooses procreation as the one respect in which he differs from men. Surely the Anglo-Saxons did not need Freud to suggest to them the phallic qualities of swords. The paradox of this metaphor is that while the penis creates life where it penetrates, the sword not only cannot create life, but it kills what it penetrates, in this case, specifically a woman's body. The reader's horror at this graphically depicted paradox induces serious thought on issues much larger than that of the nature of swords: the natural connection of virility with the generation of life, and the unnatural, socially determined connection of virility with violence.

Riddle 25 likewise deals with paradoxes of life and death with reference to sexual matters, but this riddle is playful and pleasant, and represents what one would hope were more usual sexual relations among the Anglo-Saxons. The speaker begins just as the sword did by calling himself "a wonderful thing," but unlike the sword, he is a joy to women. He stands high on a bed (which word had in Old English the same two meanings it has today—a piece of furniture for sleeping and a garden plot), and is hairy underneath. Sometimes a fair peasant's daughter grips him, red, and confines him. That curly-haired woman soon feels her meeting with him: "Wæt bið þæt eage: [Wet is that eye, 11b]. Of course, Onion is a satisfactory solution, but handsome, curly-haired maidens are not the only people who enjoy digging up onions. The persistent double-entendres comically draw a paradox: the death of the onion is the life-function of the penis. But the similarities are more in evidence than the differences. Onions and penises have in common not only some aspects of their physical appearance, but their functions of preserving life and conviviality. A good man and a good supper— what could a peasant's daughter find more congenial than these two?

Riddle 27 (Mead) takes a darker view of the power of food. This speaker, like the inkhorn of Riddle 88, begins by rehearsing his history: he is carried from groves, mountains, valleys, and hills,

borne by wings through the air, and lodged under a roof. Then men
bathe him in vats. Now he is "a binder and a scourger," throwing
both youths and old men to the floor, robbing them of their power of
mind and body, although allowing them strength of speech. The
paradox in this riddle is that the speaker is small enough to be
carried by a bee and weak enough to be bathed by a man, but strong
enough to hurl men to the floor on their backs. The description of
drunkenness is particularly vivid, and the reader can only respond
by assenting to the truth of the speaker's boasts and feeling foolish
for ever engaging such an adversary.

As a final example of the riddlic inanimate speaker, I offer an
officially unsolved riddle, number 74. It is very brief:

> Ic wæs fæmne geong,   feaxhar cwene,
> ond ænlic rinc   on ane tid;
> fleah mid fuglum   ond on flode swom,
> deaf under yþe   dead mid fiscum,
> ond on foldan stop,   hæfde ferð cwicu.

[I was a young woman, a gray-haired queen, and a peerless warrior, all at
one time. I flew with the birds, and swam in the sea, dove under the
waves dead among the fishes, and trod the earth, had a living soul.]

This speaker cuts across so many ontological categories that the
reader first assumes that, despite the initial personification, it cannot possibly be human: it is both young and old, male and female; it
is at home in the air, on and in the water, and on land; it is both dead
and alive. For a time, I understood all this figuratively, and solved
the riddle as Rain. The young woman is the spring sunshower, the
gray-haired queen is the persistent November drizzle, and the
peerless warrior is the thunderstorm. Rain flies through the air,
loses itself in the sea, and walks on the earth as the raindrops
bounce from the surface as though alive. But the consistent use of
the preterite confounds this interpretation. My favored solution now
posits a human speaker and a literal acceptance of her or his words:
the speaker can only be a poet or reader. Certainly, the poet or
reader of a group of poems like those in the Exeter Book could
speak these words with truth. This solution may not be the one
intended by its author, but it is the one that brings this riddle to life
for me, and that causes me to think most deeply about my own
experiences. Moreover, I respond to the way this solution leads the
reader not merely from human to inanimate, as do most of the first-
person riddles, but rather from human to inanimate and then back
to human again.

"The Husband's Message" concludes this discussion of the in-animate speaker. This enigmatic poem is one of several, including "The Wife's Lament," "Resignation," and "The Ruin," appearing in the Exeter Book between the two large groups of riddles. Among this small group of poems, which are distinguished from one an-other only by large initial capitals, is a second version of Riddle 30, which is followed by four sections of verse, and then by "The Ruin." The *ASPR* provides the title "Riddle 60" for the first of these four passages and groups the next three as "The Husband's Message," admitting that this decision "must depend upon the subjective judgement of the editor" (3, lxi). As it stands now, scholarly and critical opinion is split on the question of whether to include this first section in "The Husband's Message," with both early and recent scholars arguing on both sides of the question.[6] However, I find it most satisfactory to include Riddle 60 as the first section of "The Husband's Message" for reasons given below. For convenience sake, however, I refer to the lines in the *ASPR* Riddle 60 as R1, R2, etc., and to those in the sections it designates "The Husband's Message" as HM1, HM2, etc.

The poem begins, like the Inkhorn and Mead riddles, in the first person with a description of the speaker's former existence in a desolate spot by the seashore (R1–7a). It expresses wonder that it should ever have come "muðleas sprecan" [to speak without a mouth, R9b], and that it should have been cut by a knife and strong hand. The speaker thus far is certainly to be understood as a reed pen. The speaker concludes this section stating that it was cut

>   þæt ic wiþ þe sceolde
> for unc anum twam   ærendspræce
> abeodan bealdlice,   swa hit beorna ma
> uncre wordcwidas   widdor ne mænden.

>   (R14b–R17)

[so that I could boldly present the message to you in the presence of the two of us, so that more men would not more widely know our words]

The second scribal division, beginning "Nu ic onsundran þe secgan wille" [Now I wish to tell you apart, HM1], continues with the same theme and tone as the preceding passage. This line, in fact, has every indication of being a logical continuation of the sense of the preceding clause. The speaker of lines R1–17 implies that he was made into a pen in order to deliver a message in such a way that no other person would know that message (as would be the case if a

human messenger were employed), and then the first line of the next
section merely states that he will in fact deliver this secret message.
If Riddle 60 is taken as a distinct poem, one must then explain how
the riddle itself can be understood as an *ærendsprǣc* "message"
(R15b), and one must settle for an opening to the "Message" that
looks more like a continuation than a beginning. The only plausible
reason for rejecting the unity of this four-part poem would be that
the speaker of the second through fourth sections cannot be a pen,
and is usually understood to be a rune staff.[7] However, the speaker
of these sections is more satisfactorily understood to be the personified penned message. The shift in the speaker from the pen to the
message it writes is similar to the shift in Riddle 27 from pollen to
honey to mead. The written message as speaker has ample analogues in the four manuscript prefaces, and it allows a supporting
role for the rune staff that makes its appearance at the end of the
poem.

A large hole in the folio has eliminated so much of the text of the
next five lines that the complete sense is hopelessly obscure. We
find the fragment "treocyn ic tudre aweox," which is usually understood to mean something like "I, a member of the tree family, grew
from a shoot," and is thus taken as an indication of a new speaker
here who is a wooden object, but *treocynn* (which occurs nowhere
else in the poetic corpus) may mean merely "a plant," and thus
seems a slender basis for positing a new speaker, and a new poem.
In the following lines appear the words "settan" [to write], rather
than *writan* or *agrafan* "to engrave," which one would expect if the
speaker were a rune staff; "ellor londes" [of a foreign land] and
"Ful oft ic on bates" [very often I on a boat's], which must have to
do with the voyage the speaker has just made; and "mondryhten
min" [my lord], reminiscent of the *halungboc's* relationship to
Thureth and of the sword's relationship to its owner in Riddle 20.
This second scribal section concludes with the speaker's statement
that it has now come to tell "you" about his lord's love. Thus, the
speaker has greatly postponed the message proper to rehearse its
history and establish its credentials, much as the speakers of the
prefaces do, and as does the animated cross in "The Dream of the
Rood."

The message itself begins in the third scribal section as indirect
discourse—that is, it is still in the words of the speaker of the poem
rather than in those of the sender. It begins, "Hwæt, þec þonne
biddan het se þisne beam agrof" [He who engraved this piece of
wood commanded me to bid you, HM13], and it is here that the
second reference to a tree occurs, although this time the reference

is clearly to the rune staff, which must be accompanying the penned message, rather than to the speaker itself. This makes a great deal of sense in an early manuscript culture which granted scant authority to the written word and which relied on objects such as rings, staffs, or seals to verify the authenticity of the missive. In the message proper we learn that the recipient is a chieftain's daughter (HM47a) and the sender her husband or lover. The bulk of scribal sections three and four is taken up with reminders of the former intimacy between sender and recipient, instructions on how and when she is to travel to him, and assurances that he is well-off and eager to see her.

Finally in line HM49, the speaker presents the runes, and here again we are on unfirm ground. The passage reads as follows:

> Gecyre ic ætsomme · ᛋ · ᚱ · geador
> ·ᚹ·ᛈ· ond ·ᛗ· aþe benemnan
> þæt he þa wære ond þa winetreowe
> be him lifegendum læstan wolde,
> þe git on ærdagum oft gespræconn.

> (49–53)

[I put together ᛋ ᚱ ᚹ ᛈ and ᛗ to declare with an oath that he was there, and that he would carry out, while he lived, the fidelity of friends which you two often spoke of in previous days.]

There is no consensus on the interpretation of this passage. The runes, whether used as phonetic characters or as words, may have had some conventional meaning understood by the poet's readership, if not by us, or they may have spelled a name by some phonetic scheme to which we lack the key. All we can be sure of is that the runes somehow serve to authenticate the message.[8]

Despite the many obscurities that "The Message" presents, we can make several observations about its speaker. First, the speaker devotes an inordinate number of lines—29 of 70—to its own history, although such information is clearly peripheral to the message. Second, these first 29 lines of the poem (R1–HM12) are far more specific and detailed than the remaining 41 lines of the message proper, which is vague by any standards. One might compare, for example, the description the speaker gives of his original home

> Ic wæs be sonde, sæwealle neah,
> æt merefaroþe, minum gewunade
> frumstaþole fæst; fea ænig wæs

monna cynnes,   þæt minne þær
on anæde   eard beheolde,
ac mec uhtna gehwam   yð sio brune
lagufæðme beleolc.

(R1–7a)

[I was by the sand, near the sea wall, at the ocean shore, firm in my
habitual birth place. There were few men who beheld me there in the
solitary land, but the brown wave, the embrace of water, encircled me
every morning before dawn.]

with what the speaker has to say about the husband's new home,
the place to which the lady is to travel—it is merely "suð . . . ofer
merelade" [south over the sea-path, HM27b–28a]. Third, the
speaker does not actually give the message, but paraphrases it. By
rendering the message in indirect discourse, the speaker effectively
remains prominent throughout. Fourth, the speaker sprinkles its
discourse with expressions designed to keep itself in the foreground
of the reader's consciousness, such as "heht nu sylfa þe lustum
læran" [he now bids me teach you willingly, HM20b–21a] and "þæs
þe he me sægde" [as he said to me, HM31b]. Furthermore, the
speaker's relationship to the man seems to be as close, if not closer,
in its own eyes at least, as that of the woman to the man. According
to the speaker, the man is "mondryhten min" [my lord, HM7] and
"min wine" [my friend, HM39b]. In all these points the speaker of
"The Husband's Message" greatly resembles the self-important
speakers of the prosopopoeic prefaces: the special and intimate
relationship with a human master and the exorbitant praise of his
virtues, the astonishing interest in rehearsing its own history, and
the highly exaggerated sense of its own importance. Perhaps a more
appropriate title for this poem would have been "The Husband's
Messenger."

Some scholars find Christian allegory in "The Husband's Message," but although each presents a thoughtful reading, none is
convincing.[9] Aside from the problems each of these allegorical
readings creates, the poem works very well just as it is. Despite its
inanimate speaker, which indicates proximity to oral culture, this is
truly a very literary poem, for it focuses not on the characters of the
two lovers, nor on their story, but on the message itself, on the
written medium by which it was possible for two literate people to
communicate over long distances "swa hit beorna ma uncre word-
cwidas widdor ne mænden." This poem seems to be something of a

novelty, a light-hearted experiment in focusing on the unexpected role of literacy in a sexual relationship, and in this light-heartedness it reminds one of many of the riddles. The prosopopoeic speaker in "The Dream of the Rood," taken up in the final chapter, returns this type of speaker to the role of earnest witness that it plays in the prefaces, leaving the "Message" something of an anomaly in the extant poetic corpus.

3

The Adoptable Speaker

In the discussion of lyric poems in part I, we saw that Jakobson distinguishes between poems focused on the addresser and those focused on the addressee. The first he calls lyrics and the second, prayers and charms. These two kinds of discourse are distinguished from a third kind, narrative and didactic works, which refer to a constructed world outside the I-You relationship. Thus prayers and charms, like lyric poems, but unlike narrative and didactic poems, take place entirely within the I-You relationship. Prayers and charms do differ somewhat from other kinds of lyric poems, however. For one thing, the speakers of other lyric poems may pretend to have no audience, often speaking in an overheard monologue or an apostrophe. In these poems, as Jakobson points out, the set is on the speaker, not on the addressee. However, such lyric poems do have an implicit addressee—the reader—who is expected to engage in the speaker's thoughts and emotions, and in some lyrics the speaker reaches out to his audience by using the first-person plural, as Caedmon does, or by mentioning the cultural group to which he expects his audience to belong, as in "The Battle of Brunanburh" (see chapter 4).

In prayers and charms, however, this situation is reversed. Rather than a specific speaker expecting to be overheard by a generally defined audience, we have a specific addressee addressed by anyone who is interested in speaking the poem. In other words, the poem's "I" is adoptable by the reader—any reader who finds it suitable to do so. The speaker may very well be expressing the thoughts and emotions of the poet, but when a poet troubles to write down a prayer, or teach it orally to someone else, she expects that the reader or auditor will assume her role as speaker. The reader's engagement with the speaker therefore becomes an actual adoption of the speaker's words for the reader's own. In prayers and charms, the empathetic identification of the reader with the speaker is complete.

I have been referring to prayers and charms for want of a single

word that encompasses both, but most anthropologists and lin-
guists do distinguish them thus: the prayer supplicates a spirit or
deity to bring about an act in accordance with the wishes expressed
by the speaker, while a charm actually effects the desired result
without the intervention of any spiritual third party.[1] Jakobson uses
the terms "supplicatory" for prayers and "exhortative" for charms:
the distinction rests in whether the speaker is subordinate to the
addressee, as in the prayer, or the addressee is subordinate to the
speaker, as in the charm. In short, prayers ask; charms act. Of
course, as is obvious to anyone who has read through the Old
English metrical charms, the religious element appears frequently,
and often it is impossible to separate the religious from the magical,
the supplication from the exhortation.

"A Prayer" is a 79-line poem written in a twelfth-century manuscript, where it follows Ælfric's Grammar and Glossary, and also, in
a fragmentary form, in the eleventh-century Lambeth Psalter. The
first 55 lines comprise a rather generally stated supplication for
mercy, which is begun with and punctuated by variations on a
formula: "Æla, drihten leof! Æla, dema god!" [O, dear Lord! O,
God the Judge! 1]; "Æla frea beorhta, folkes scippend!" [O, bright
Master, the folk's Creator! 8]; and "Æla, leohtes leoht! Æla, lyfes
wynn!" [O, light's Light! O, life's Joy! 21] These lines are followed by
a credo that states the speaker's subordinate relationship with God:

> Ic þe andette,   ælmightig god,
> þæt ic gelyfe on þe,   leofa hælend,
> þæt þu eart se miccla   and se mægenstranga
> and se eadmoda   ealra goda
> and se ece kyning   ealra gesceafta,
> and ic eom se litla for þe   and se lyðra man,
> se her syngige   swiðe genehhe,
> dæges and nihtes   do, swa ic ne sceolde,
> hwile mid weorc,   hwile mid worde,
> hwile mid geþohte,   þearle scyldi,
> inwitniðas   oft and gelome.

(56–66)

[I vow to you, almighty God, that I believe in you, dear Savior, that you
are the greatest and the strongest and the most benevolent of all gods
and the eternal King of all creation, and I am the little one before you,
and the baser being, who, sinning here very often by day and night, do
cunning hostilities (as I should not, at times in deeds, at times in words,
at times in thought, with heavy offense) often and frequently.]

The prayer ends with the speaker imploring God for help in working the Almighty's will and for a place in heaven.

The speaker of "A Prayer" defines himself only as one of "men ofer moldan" [people on earth, 32], and as a believer in one God who was born of a virgin in Bethlehem (45–50). (Oddly enough, the Christian speaker does recognize other lesser, weaker, and less benevolent gods in lines 58–59.) None of the other references to himself—his sinfulness, wretchedness, and hopes of heaven—differentiate him from any other living Christian. This is a prayer that can be spoken by woman or man, lord, freeman, or slave. The adoptable speaker expends his energies on emphasizing God's greatness and uniqueness and his own weakness and typicality in an effort to convince God to help him do right and to grant him mercy.

A 68-line fragment that I call "The Penitent's Prayer" uses similar techniques. This poem is found in the text of "Resignation" in the *ASPR* Exeter Book. Alan Bliss and Allen J. Frantzen, in their 1976 article on "The Integrity of *Resignation,*" have established beyond any reasonable doubt that the text designated "Resignation" in the *ASPR* is a conflation of the beginning of one poem, a prayer, and the end of another, a fictive lyric, caused by the loss of a leaf in the Exeter Book between folios 118 and 119—that is, between lines 68 and 69 of the *ASPR* text. Bliss and Frantzen designate the lines 1–68 "Resignation A," but a new title is clearly called for. "The Penitent's Prayer," an alternate title for "Resignation" as a whole, is appropriate for this fragment, and I use it here.

"A Penitent's Prayer" is not so mnemonically organized as "A Prayer," nor does it contain any striking devices of oral rhetoric like the latter's "Æla" lines. The poem begins oddly with God in the third person: "Age mec se ælmihta god, helpe min se halga dryhten! [May the almighty God deliver me, may the holy Lord help me! 1–2a]. From here on, however, God is addressed as "you." To summarize: You are great, and I commend myself to you. Show me how I can do your will. Overlook my sins, grant me patience and understanding in the trial you send me, and grant me eternal bliss. I must leave this world in a short time. You are my help, although I previously earned little honor [with you?]. Protect me and confuse the devils who want to lead me to hell. Although you gave me many honors on this earth, I am afraid for my soul because it is stained with sin.

The speaker of "A Penitent's Prayer" is more narrowly defined than the speaker of "A Prayer," who, as we have seen, could be any Christian. The speaker of "A Prayer" calls himself sinful, but this is merely the Christian notion of the human condition, there being no indication that the speaker has been especially wayward. The penitent of this prayer, however, indicates that he has previously done little—or nothing, if we take 48b–49a as litotes—to earn God's favor. Further particulars are the references to approaching death (41–43a) and to worldly honors (66b–67a). It is not surprising that the speaker of "A Prayer," which bears more of the markings of oral poetry and which was probably widely known since it is extant in two manuscripts, should be more widely adoptable than the speaker of the more literary "A Penitent's Prayer," which appears in the *mycel englisc boc* that contains many of the most highly literary poems extant. In other words, for a prayer to be preserved in an oral culture, it would have to be very widely adoptable, but that restriction is obviated for cultures that learn their prayers from books.

The two charms that I want to discuss here, sections of "For Unfruitful Land" and "A Journey Charm," are metrically deficient but highly poetic, especially in their use of metaphor, which is noticeably absent from the two prayers. "For Unfruitful Land" is in two parts, the first part (lines 1–44) for pasture and the second (45–82) for cultivated land. This second part contains, besides prose directions for placing seed in a plow, placing a loaf under the first furrow, and so on, poetic addresses to the earth. The first one begins:

> Erce, Erce, Erce   eorþan modor,
> geunne þe se alwalda,   ece drihten,
> æcera wexendra   and wridendra,
> eacniendra   and elniendra,
> sceafta hehra,   scirra wæstma

(49–55)

[Erce, Erce, Erce, Earth's mother, may the All-powerful, the eternal Lord, grant you fields waxing and flourishing, bringing forth, and strengthening shafts of millet, shining crops.]

The second address reads in full:

> Hal wes þu, folde,   fira modor!
> Beo þu growende   on godes fæþme,
> fodre gefylled   firum to nytte.

(69–71)

[Be well, Earth, mother of men. Grow in God's embrace, filled with food for the use of men.]

The identity of "Erce, Earth's mother" is unknown. *Erce* is clearly not an Old English word, and is probably Celtic in origin.[2] In any case, Erce and her daughter Earth are personified as women who are God's, or a god's, consort, the offspring of their union being the crops. The word *eacniendra,* in the first poem, which I have translated "bringing forth," is usually found modifying mortal women and means, simply, "pregnant." *Wæstm,* which I translated "crops" because the references are to grain, has the general meaning "fruit" and when used of humans means "offspring." So, to follow through with the personification, we can summarize these lines thus: "Erce, Earth's mother, may God grant you pregnant fields and shining offspring." In the second poem, the word *fæþm,* which I translated "embrace," may also mean "bosom" or "lap," and the lines "Grow in God's embrace, filled with food" likewise suggest human sexual activity and reproduction. The speaker of these poems—who is probably the farmer but perhaps a priest, wisewoman, or other professional—communicates with the Earth in human terms. By personifying her, he reduces her mysterious ways of producing crops to terms that he can understand. In so doing, he breaks down the taxonomic walls both between animate and inanimate and between human and divine, thus empathetically identifying with her—and producing some beautiful poetry.

"A Journey Charm" is a 42-line poem that, like the poems in "For Unfruitful Land," employs a structural metaphor to transcend the boundaries between the human and the divine. Unlike these poems, however, it is wholly Christian. The speaker, who is adoptable by any traveler, begins by stating that he protects himself with a staff and commends himself to God, both of which—the staff and God—will protect him from the dangers of travel. "Sygegealdor ic begale, sigegyrd ic me wege, wordsige and worcsige" [A victory-song I sing, a victory-staff I carry, word-victory and deed-victory, 6–7a] This sentence sets up the analogy between the poem itself—the *sygegealdor*—and an object that provides physical protection—the staff. Following this is a listing of biblical figures, obscured by the loss of two half-lines of verse from our text:

> ac gehæle me ælmihtig and sunu   and frofre gast,
> ealles wuldres   wyrðig dryhten,
> swa swa ic gehyrde   heofna scyppende.
> [* * *]   Abrame and Isace
> and swilce men,   Moyses and Iacob,
> and Dauit and Iosep   [* * *]
> and Evan and Annan   and Elizabet,

Saharie and ec Marie,   modur Cristes
and eac þæ gebroþru,   Petrus and Paulus.

(10–18)

[but may the Almighty and the Son and the Holy Ghost keep me well, the exalted Lord of all glory, as I heard the Creator of the heavens * * * Abraham and Isaac and such men, Moses and Jacob, and David and Joseph * * * and Eve and Anne and Elizabeth, Sarah and also Mary, Christ's mother, and also the brothers Peter and Paul.

The best sense that can be made of this passage is that the speaker is requesting the same protection that he knows God gave to all these people. The speaker wishes to include himself in their number by identifying with them. Certainly God "kept well" Abraham, Isaac, Moses, Jacob, David, Joseph (whether St. Joseph or Jacob's son), Anne, Elizabeth, Sarah, Mary, Peter (despite his martyrdom), and Paul, but what of Eve? That so many women should be included in this list is also peculiar given the male slant of the bulk of Anglo-Saxon poetry and of this poem in particular, which focuses in the lines to come on God as Germanic warlord. Perhaps the women are included as a means of making this poem more adoptable by women, who, as travelers, had at least as much need of protection as men. The women, including the inappropriate Eve, thus serve to extend the poem to women speakers.

The poem continues:

```
                    si me wuldres hyht,
        hand ofer heafod,      haligra rof,
        sigerofra sceolu,      soðfæstra engla.
        Biddu ealle   bliðu mode
        þæt me beo Matheus helm,      Marcus byrne,
        leoht, lifes rof,      Lucos min swurd,
        scearp and scirecg,      scyld Iohannes,
        wuldre gewlitegod      wælgar Serafhin.
```

(23b–30)

[May the hope of glory be for me a hand over my head, a roof of saints, a troop of victorious, righteous angels. I pray to all with blithe thought that Matthew be my helm; Mark my byrnie, the bright covering of life; Luke my sword, sharp and shining-edged; John my shield, made beautiful in glory; the seraphim my slaughter-spear]

The poem ends with a request that the speaker might dwell in God's peace, *belocun*, literally, "locked up" against the foe, *gestapelod* "stationed" in the glory of the angels (39–40). This entire passage is a large-scale working out of the commonly used Anglo-Saxon metaphor for God as a Germanic warrior-chief. The "hand ofer heafod" [hand over my head, 24] may be seen in general as the protecting hand of God, analogous to the "haligra rof" [roof of saints] in the same line, but it is also, and more specifically, a reference to God as comitatus lord, and to the custom of the lord's placing his hand on the thane's head during pledging or gift-giving. Like the popular Protestant hymn "Onward Christian Soldiers," this passage places the speaker amongst warriors led by God, and further metaphorizes the Evangelists and seraphim as his armor and weapons.[3] The speaker's relationship to the addressee, God, is both conventional and metaphorical. As in the poems in "For Unfruitful Land," this speaker addresses the deity in human terms, reducing the divine mystery of God's protection to the human world of weapons and armor and membership in the Anglo-Saxon comitatus. Addressed in this way, God is brought close to the speaker, into his world.

These four poems addressing a deity and employing a speaker who is more or less adoptable by anyone whose circumstances suit the poem, are not as artistically sophisticated as are at least some of the poems using other kinds of speakers. There seems to be no good reason why this should necessarily be true, but perhaps it is so because prayers and charms have some value beyond any literary merit, and therefore are worth preserving even if they are artistically naive. Nevertheless, the transcendent metaphors employed in the two charms do endow them with aesthetic interest.

4

The Nonpersonal Speaker

As we saw in the first chapter, a lyric poem need not employ the first-person singular pronoun in order to engage the reader in the I-You world. These poems, uttered without an "I," are often styled "impersonal," but that term is misleading because it denotes "exhibiting no emotion or personality." Such a work would clearly not be a lyric poem. Therefore, I call such lyrics "nonpersonal," by which I mean that the speaker is not explicitly presented as a persona, but that, although there is no "I," the speaker is nevertheless present in her or his utterance and is responding emotionally to his or her topic. Nonpersonal poems require modern readers to work harder in our readings, because we find it troubling to be confronted with a lyric poem in which the speaker's identity is not readily apparent even as a pronoun.

Among the lyrics of the Exeter Book, only "The Ruin" uses the nonpersonal voice; many of the remaining examples of nonpersonal lyrics are found embedded in prose texts and are firmly datable to either the extreme beginning or end of the Anglo-Saxon literary period. One might consequently conclude that the nonpersonal voice was an anomaly in the Old English lyric tradition, but, given the small number of surviving manuscripts, this conclusion is not supportable. It is more probable that the poems of the Exeter Book were chosen under some principle of selection unknown to us, which may have favored lyrics using a fictive "I," to the near exclusion of a body of nonpersonal lyrics. Although it remains impossible to say just how popular the nonpersonal voice was among Anglo-Saxon writers and readers of lyric poetry, we can properly see the contextual evidence as an indication of widespread use. That is, we can say with certainty that the nonpersonal voice was employed in poems dating from the very beginning to the very end of the period—from "Caedmon's Hymn" in the seventh century to "Durham" in the twelfth—and that these poems were included in a wide variety of contexts—"The Ruin" in a verse anthology, "Durham" and "The Kentish Hymn" in miscellaneous volumes, "The

Father's Lament" (*Beowulf* 2444–62a) in an epic poem, "Caedmon's Hymn" in a prose historical narrative, and the others as
entries in *The Anglo-Saxon Chronicle*.

Many of these nonpersonal poems have been criticized for lack
of artistic competence, or compared unfavorably to other poems
that seem to modern critics to be companion pieces. For example,
"The Battle of Brunanburh" is sometimes felt to be more impersonal, and thus less successful, than "The Battle of Maldon,"
which is a lay rather than a lyric and therefore not a comparable
poem; "The Ruin" is sometimes felt to be more impersonal, and
thus less profound, than "The Wanderer" and "The Seafarer," two
fictive lyrics on a far different topic; and "The Father's Lament" is
often criticized as conventional relative to independent lyrics using
the image of the deserted mead hall, such as "The Ruin" and "The
Wanderer." However, many of these poems are eminently successful pieces when examined on their own terms, and their success is at least partially attributable to their effective use of the
nonpersonal voice.

Caedmon's only known extant work is the 9-line lyric found in
seventeen manuscripts of Bede's *Ecclesiastical History*. Although
"Caedmon's Hymn" was first sung as an impromptu solo, the plural
verb in "Nu sculon herigean" [Now we ought to praise, 1a] indicates that the poem is in fact a hymn—"a lyric poem expressing
religious emotion and generally intended to be sung by a cho-
rus"[1]—and suggests that the speaker is here a spokesman for
humanity. The identification of the implied subject of the sentence
as "humanity" bears on the interpretation of the poem as a whole.
The speaker of "Caedmon's Hymn" twice makes humanity the
indirect object of God's act of creation. In lines 5–6, the speaker
tells us that God "ærest sceop eorðan bearnum heofon to hrofe"
[first created heaven as a roof for the children of earth], then, in
lines 7–9, that "middangeard . . . æfter teode firum foldan" [later
he made earth for the men of the world]. To imply that heaven and
earth were made for us, rather than that we were made for God's
creation, does not constitute a good paraphrase of Genesis,[2] but
this twofold emphasis on humanity in the "Hymn" has a point: the
same point as that of the choice of the plural verb. Caedmon's
theme here is the reciprocal relationship between humanity and its
creator: to summarize the poem, "We will praise God because he
made heaven and earth for us." Thus, Caedmon's decision to es-
chew his own voice in this poem was well grounded—and successful. Whatever we may think of the poem's artistic merit, it
seems to have been immensely popular in Anglo-Saxon England,

and was certainly considered some sort of paradigm or archetype of all the poetry written after it. The choice of the non-personal voice is integral to Caedmon's theme, and thus the "Hymn" presents a small but telling example of the sophistication, and success, with which this voice could be used.

"Durham" is a much different lyric poem, one that can be justly called minor in both the aesthetic and the historical senses. If "Durham" is merely a schoolboy exercise in the classical rhetorical mode of the *encomium urbis,* that would adequately account for its lack of success in general, but the existence of a Latin prose account of Durham's relics, in the *Capitula de Miraculis et Translationibus Sancti Cuthberti,* written in the first-person voice of an eyewitness, further suggests that the unfortunate choice of the nonpersonal voice for "Durham" was the Anglo-Saxon author's own idea of a proper lyric speaker.[3]

The speaker seems to take the unusual stance of going out of his way to imply that if he has ever been to Durham at all, he does not praise the city on the basis of his first-hand knowledge, but rather on what he has learned of it in books. First, the movement from one point of view to the next is not a natural one. The poem begins with a view of the city from a distance: it is "steppa gestaðolad" [firmly built on high, 2a] and surrounded by the Wear. In line 5, however, the speaker and readers seem suddenly to be plunged into that river for a closeup view of the "feola fisca kyn on flode gemonge" [many kinds of fish in the mingling of water]. Then just as suddenly, we are again far from the city walls, noting the "countless number of wild animals" in the "deep dales" of the surrounding countryside. With line 9, we lose all sense of spatial point of view as the list of Durham's relics is rehearsed: it is not until line 18 that we learn that these relics are kept in Durham's new cathedral, surely the most important feature of the city, and probably the reason that the poem was written. Thus, the shifting point of view seems to follow no special design, whether spatial or chronological, unless it be that of the exercise itself. A second indication of a distant speaker is the mere listing of the relics: there is no sense that the speaker even knows exactly what they are let alone that he has seen them himself, as the speaker of the Latin *Translatio* has. Moreover, the speaker actually attributes his knowledge of Durham's relics to a piece of writing: "ðes ðe writ seggeð" [as the writ says, 20]. Just what this "writ" is is not certain. It is probably not the Latin *Translatio,* since this work likewise makes reference to a written authority ("ut in veteribus libris legitur"). Whether this disclaimer in the lyric is the result of a verbatim translation from the *Translatio* or of a *pro forma* insertion, it is certainly fair to say that "Durham" is an extremely bookish poem. For example, that Bede is called "breoma bocera" [famous scholar, 15] indicates that the poet was a scholar himself, for among what other group of people would Bede have been famous? The author of "Durham" eschewed the more natural first-person voice for this piece—the voice chosen by the author of the Latin work on the same subject—and instead adopted every device at his command to distance himself from his subject. Unlike Caedmon, however, this author has failed to produce a poem of much value: "Caedmon's Hymn" purposefully employs the non-personal voice in order to integrate the poet's speaker with the poet's theme, while "Durham" employs the same sort of speaker at the expense of the integrity of theme and voice. As a lyric, "Durham" is a dismal failure: it is difficult to imagine any reader catching some enthusiasm for the city from a reading of this poem.

Having examined the extremes of success and failure of the non-personal voice in two short and aesthetically minor lyrics, I now turn to the six poems included in *The Anglo-Saxon Chronicle,* which, as a group, are uneven at best. Although the chronicles are unsigned, their authors were connected in some way with the secular administration of Wessex.[4] In examining the speakers of these six lyrics, then, we should keep in mind the location and loyalties of the authors, the likelihood that they felt bound to adopt the non-personal voice in the context of the *Chronicle,* and the close identification that their contemporary readers must have made between the speakers of the poems and the chronicler-poets.

Although "The Battle of Brunanburh" is the earliest of the six *Chronicle* poems, it is by far the most sophisticated, and is therefore reserved till last in this discussion. Each of the other five may be thought of as lyrics of some sort, whether panegyrics or descriptive pieces, but not all of them are successful in conveying the emotional response of the speaker to his topic. "The Coronation of Edgar," for example, might have concerned itself more with praise or description rather than with versifying the date of the coronation over some ten of its twenty lines. The speaker of this piece is indeed so timid that not only does he take the date of the coronation as his topic, but he makes two disclaimers—"mine gefrege" [according to my information, 9b] and "þæs ðe gewritu secgað" [this the writings say, 14]—the second of which clears him of responsibility for the laboriously presented date. The speakers of "The Death of Alfred" and "The Death of Edward," on the other hand, err on the side of zeal rather than circumspection by sprinkling ethical modifiers such as "yfel" [evil] and "clæne and milde" [pure and gentle] throughout poems having to do with political instability. These speakers establish themselves as men who hold strong opinions on the subject of the goodness of the royal line—whichever royal line is currently in power. Comparing the two poems is instructive: Earl Godwine is the villain in "Death of Alfred," written during Ethelred's reign, but twenty-nine years later in "Death of Edward," Godwine's son, Harold Godwinsson, the new English king, is called *æþele,* an adjective that implies noble birth. Yet the prudent speaker of "Coronation" and the yea-saying speakers of "Death of Alfred" and "Death of Edward" are more alike than different, for each of these three speakers adopts the chronicler's stance, the point of view of the *bocere* "scribe or scholar" under royal patronage. The use of the non-personal voice helps to establish the official, rather than personal, identity of the speaker.

Two other of the *Chronicle* poems are somewhat more rewarding in that the speaker of each has, in his control over the material, something of the auctorial, as well as the authoritative, about him. "The Capture of the Five Boroughs" demonstrates both a formal and a lexical pattern. The formal pattern is a kind of closure, unusual in Old English poetry, in which the last verse repeats the first, and both state the subject, "Eadmund cyning."[5] The lexical pattern has to do with the alignment of words for movement and containment. The text of the entire poem is given below with the pertinent words in italics.

> Her Eadmund cyning,   Engla þeoden,
> mæcgea mundbora,   Myrce *geeode,*
> dyre *dædfruma,*   swa Dor *scadeþ,*
> Hwitanwyllesgeat,   and Humbra ea,
> 5 brada brimstream.   Burga fife,
> Ligoraceaster   and Lincylene
> and Snotingaham,   swylce Stanford eac
> and Deoraby.   Dæne wæran æror
> under Norðmannum   nyde *gebegde*
> 10 on hæþenra   *hæfteclommum*
> lange þrage,   oþ hie *alysde* eft
> for his weorþscipe   wiggendra hleo,
> afera Eadweardes,   Eadmund cyning.

[In this year King Edmund, prince of the Angles, protector of kinsmen, noble *doer of deeds, overran* Mercia, where the Dor, the Hwitanwyllesgeat, and the River Humber *bound* the five boroughs—Leicester and Lincoln and Nottingham, likewise Stamford and Derby. The Danes were previously under the Northmen, *subdued* by force, in the heathens' *fetters* for a long time, until King Edmund, the shelter of warriors, the heir of Edward, *freed* them then for his honor.]

All the words having to do with movement are used in connection with Edmund: *geeode* "overran" *dædfruma* "doer of deeds," *alysde* "freed." Likewise, all the words having to do with containment are used in connection with the captive five boroughs: *scadeþ* "bound" by the three rivers, *gebegde* "subdued," and *on hæfteclommum* "in fetters"—the last of which is, of course, metaphoric. This pattern of movement and containment presents a clear picture of Edmund moving into an enclosed space and liberating it: clearly, the poem should be titled "The *Freeing* of the Five Boroughs," since in the mind of this speaker it is the Vikings who *capture* cities and the English who *free* them.

The speaker of "The Death of Edgar" likewise appears as a man with some aesthetic ambition, which is obscured for modern readers by an unfortunate title: "The Disasters of 975" would be more comprehensive, and at the same time indicative of the structure of this incrementally patterned poem. The poem falls naturally into six sections: lines 1–12 deal with the death of King Edgar, lines 13–15 with the death of Bishop Cyneweard, 16–23 with the breaking up of the monasteries, 24–28 with the driving out of a certain Oslac, 29–33a with the appearance of a comet, and 33b–37 with a famine.[6] The first four sections share a common theme, since all deal with death or destruction. We can feel certain that the speaker is aware of this connection and that he did not just gather these four events together in verse because they all happened in the same year, since in each of these first four sections we find images of breaking up, of movement away from the center. The speaker starts out slowly with this theme, first saying that Edgar *forlet* "left behind" his life, and that Cyneweard *gewat* "departed" from Britain. Already there is the sense of the speaker as one left behind in a world much the worse for these losses. The poet picks up the speed of this pattern in the third section: here, many monks are *todræfed* 'driven out,' and man *tobræc* "broke to pieces" God's law. Here, the recurrence of the prefix *to-* "asunder" increases the reader's sense of fragmentation. Then in the fourth section, we read that Oslac was *adræfed* "driven away" from the country, *bereafod* "robbed" of his home, both of which verbs share the sense of separating two elements that belong together—Oslac and his homeland. Clearly, the speaker presents a picture of violent breakup, of great commotion, and of himself as one who is left in the incresingly empty center. The appearance of the comet, presented in the fifth section, supports this theme of movement and of things out of their proper place. The ending of the poem, however, is weak. The poet presents the famine as God's vengeance, and the return of the fruits of the earth as his making amends for the famine. The positive note on which the poem ends seems unconvincing to the reader who has followed the pattern of break-up through the first 33 lines. Nothing else has been resolved: Edgar has been succeeded by a "cild unweaxen" [an ungrown child, 11b], Cyneweard's bishopric seems to remain unfilled, the monasteries have not been repeopled, nor has Oslac been avenged, and the comet is still in the sky. It seems that the poet chose the only positive note available to him as a chronicler, the end of the famine, on which to conclude his unhappy subject.

The five minor *Chronicle* poems, then, each present a fairly well defined non-personal voice. In "Coronation of Edgar" we clearly hear the circumspect chronicler and in "Death of Alfred" and "Death of Edward" we just as clearly hear the ebullient chronicler. About these three poems, we can say that the lack of success they exhibit has more to do with their authors' lack of artistic competence than with the distance between speaker and topic, which, however, is very great. "Five Boroughs" and "Death of Edgar," on the other hand, achieve some measure of success through the control their speakers have over the material, despite an equally great distance between speaker and topic. Both of these poems thus succeed in engaging the reader in an identification with the speaker and his emotional response to the topic. We rejoice with the speaker of "Five Boroughs" and feel the desolation of the speaker of "Death of Edgar."

"The Battle of Brunanburh," unlike any of the lyrics discussed up to this point, is almost universally acknowledged as a moving lyric poem, that is, a poem that successfully conveys its speaker's emotional response to his subject. Nevertheless, many critics have faulted the poet for his lack of involvement in his subject. Dobbie, for example, states that "the poet seems to know little, and care less, of the actual course of events, but gives full play to his feelings of exultation at the victory over a foreign foe" (*ASPR* VI, xl). It may well be that the poet was in ignorance of the actual course of events, but this can never be known: despite its inclusion in the *Chronicle*, the piece is a lyric poem, not a news report, and we are told as much of the story as we need to know to involve ourselves in the emotion of the speaker. In addition, whatever the poet may or may not know, the speaker seems to know a great deal—more, in fact, than would have been possible for an eyewitness. He knows, for example, that Anlaf was fated (epic narrators know such things about their characters, but this knowledge seems unusual for a lyric speaker), that the Northmen were ashamed at their defeat, that they returned to Dublin (rather than, perhaps, trying their luck elsewhere), and that the raven, eagle, and wolf enjoyed the carrion after the survivors left (he is even able to describe the eagle so that its species is identifiable[7]). And finally, he knows the military history of the Anglo-Saxons since the time of the migration almost four hundred years earlier. Thus, the speaker represents himself here and there in the poem as an authority, more an authority than any eyewitness could have been, for he, the speaker, is both omniscient and in total control of the chronology of the battle and its aftermath. In other words, the narrative backdrop as we have it exists solely in the mind of the speaker.

The speaker's control of the structure of the poem contributes to the development of his persona. The first sentence could almost be called a thesis statement:

> Her Æþelstan cyning,   eorla dryhten,
> beorna beahgifa,   and his broþor eac,
> Eadmund æþeling,   ealdorlangne tir
> geslogon æt sæcce   sweorda ecgum
> ymbe Brunanburh.

[In this year King Athelstan, lord of earls, ring-giver of warriors, and also his brother, Prince Edmund, won age-long glory with the edges of swords in battle around Brunanburh.]

The last sentence of the poem could pass as a restatement of that thesis in a larger context:

> Ne wearð wæl mare
> on þis eigland   æfre gieta
> folces gefylled   beforan þissum
> sweordes ecgum,   þæs þe us secgað bec,
> ealde uðwitan,   siþþan eastan hider
> Engle and Seaxe   up becoman,
> ofer brad brimu   Brytene sohtan,
> wlance wigsmiþas,   Wealas ofercoman,
> eorlas arhwate   eard begeatan.

(65b–73)

[There was never greater slaughter on this island, felling of a people with the edges of swords, since the Angles and Saxons, the proud war-smiths, earls eager for glory, came hither from the east, sought Britain over the broad sea, conquered Wales and obtained the homeland.]

This is as expert an instance of closure as one is likely to find in Old English literature. But in addition, it is also an important factor in establishing an omniscient yet closeted speaker, a speaker who has the ability and leisure to re-form the raw material of the victory into a lyric poem.

A second distinctive attribute of this speaker is his ability to control chronology, which is an important feature in two other non-personal poems, "The Ruin" and "The Father's Lament," just as it is in the major fictive lyrics, although it does not appear in the shorter non-personal poems we have been examining. One example of this speaker's ability to present his own concept of time in the battle is the often quoted clause concerning the sun:

> siðþan sunne up
> on morgentid,   mære tungol,
> glad ofer grundas,   godes condel beorht,
> eces drihtnes,   oð sio æþele gesceaft
> sah to setle.

(13b–17a)

[since the sun came up in the morning—the glorious star, the bright candle of God the eternal lord—and glided over the ground, until the noble creation sank to its seat]

This clause, which is a poetic periphrasis for "all day," works so well precisely because it is so long: the sun comes up in the first verse and sinks only in the last. The structure of this periodic clause echoes the sense: the day of battle seems a long time indeed to the reader who must wade through four periphrastic expressions ("glorious star," "noble creature," "God's bright candle," and "eternal lord") as well as the connotation of slowness in the verb 'glide' before he arrives at sunset. This sense of the immense length of time during which this slaughter was carried out is echoed in line 21 with the phrase "ondlongne dæg" [all day long], in which *ondlong* indicates "far-stretching" (*OED* s.v. "along"). The speaker has chosen a most successful way to indicate time lyrically—in fact, he is so successful in giving the impression that the battle lasted from dawn to dusk that the reader fails to wonder why this should be if indeed the victory was as easy as the speaker states that it was.

Another way in which the speaker controls time in the poem is his technique of focussing on the antecedents and consequences of the battle.[8] For example, the expression "beorna beahgifa" [the ring-giver of warriors, 2a], although surely conventional, suggests a mental picture of King Athelstan in his hall, fulfilling his peace-time duties. This image fits well with the theme of its context in the first ten lines of the poem, which introduce the concept of the king's noble lineage and mention both his father and his brother. A more obvious example of the same technique occurs in the poet's treatment of the enemy forces, who are called "þæra þe mid Anlafe ofer æra gebland on lides bosme land gesohtun" [those who with Anlaf sought land over the sea surge, on the deck of a ship, 26–27], rather than merely "those who fought with Anlaf." After all, the travel arrangements of the Norwegians and Scots are irrelevant to the narrative background: if they are introduced at all, it must be either to show the speaker's omniscience, or to achieve the effect of the speaker's concept of time as flexible rather than rigidly linear, or both. A third example of the poet's ability to make the past present is in the two references to swords: "hamora lafan" [leavings of hammers, 6b] and "mylenscearpan" [mill-sharp, 24a]. Rather than serving merely in the first instance to periphrase or in the second instance to describe the swords, both expressions have the additional function of bringing the history of the swords into the present moment of the battle. The manufacture of the Mercians' weapons is just as irrelevant to the narrative as the manner of the Vikings' arrival, but the introduction of this idea serves again to show the flexibility of time in the mind of the speaker. One of these instances alone might be understood as conventional and coincidental, but the two together indicate a speaker in control of his subject.

The speaker turns from antecedents to consequences in line 32 when he begins to describe the flight of the enemy. There are many references in this part of the poem to the enemy's departure by ship, all of which represent details which the poet could not possibly know for facts, but they are all in the section of the poem that uses as narrative background the flight of the Northmen, so they are proper here and represent omniscience rather than manipulation of time. However, the well-known three-part repetend of "hreman ne þorfte" [he did not need to boast, 39b], "Gelpan ne þorfte" [he did not need to exult, 44b], and "hlehhan ne þorftun" [they did not need to laugh, 47b] does represent such a projection into the future. In other words, in describing the flight of the Northmen, the speaker realizes for his readers the future that these warriors will have to face upon return to their families: the consequences of the battle that lie days or even years ahead are made present in the poem at the time of their departure.

Third, the speaker controls point of view in the poem. Shifting point of view is, of course, the prerogative of the omniscient third-person speaker, but this device can either conceal the speaker, as in "Durham," or make the reader acutely aware of him: the speaker of "Brunanburh" uses shifting point of view to place himself for his readers. A quick look over the poem reveals that the point of view in time remains throughout in the future, relative to the present of the events described. Fixing the point of view spatially, however, is a little more difficult. Some critics have found the speaker present on the battle field.[9] Surely, the reader feels herself there, but a close examination of the poem reveals that the speaker is not *in situ*. If the speaker could be said to be pictured as having any spatial position at all (other than behind a desk many miles away) it must be that he presents a bird's eye view of the battle. He can see the West Saxons pursuing the enemy (presumably to some distance, since they do so "all day"): he can see as far as the ocean in one direction and quite some way toward Wessex in the other. The description of the beasts of battle does not imply an *in situ* point of view either—in fact, it seems improbable that any one at all, let alone the speaker, is present and alive on the ground. The only close-up visual detail in the entire poem is in the description of the eagle mentioned above, the "earn æftan hwit" [white-tailed eagle, 63a]. Of course one would not wish to imply that the poet deliberately selected an aerial point of view for this poem, but it is hard to resist the impression that the speaker is somewhere up above the scene. The point is that he is not actually *in situ* at all: the sense of an aerial point of view is achieved by his bird's eye view of time, more than of space. If the reader seems to be present on the scene, it is not because the speaker is there, but because he is successful in recreating the battle.

The key to identifying the speaker's actual point of view is his remark on the migration, that "þæs þe us secgað bec, ealde uðwitan" [books tell us this, old scholars, 68b–69a]. This personification suggests that the books are old scholars for the speaker, for they contain the voices of his predecessors, scholars long since dead. The books here are specifically the volumes of *The Anglo-Saxon Chronicle* in which our speaker is writing on a fresh leaf (Bolton " 'Variation' " 370). As we saw in Chapter One, manuscript books (like the *Chronicle*) were not so fully separable from their authors as printed books are, and furthermore, the habit of reading aloud must have contributed to the relative lack of distance between the authors and readers of a manuscript book. For these reasons, the Anglo-Saxons may not have understood the phrase "bec, ealde uðwitan" as a personification at all, since in order to perceive a metaphor one must recognize an ontological gap between tenor ("bec") and vehicle ("uðwitan"). The landscape of this poem is the interior of the scriptorium, then, or perhaps one should say the interior of the mind of a poet sitting surrounded by his books and writing in the *Chronicle*. The poet takes his own point of view in space and time, and makes no secret of his speaker's identity. That he has succeeded so well in conveying his emotional response on the subject of the English victory has more to do with his skill in conveying an immediacy of feeling than with any supposed immediacy of point of view, which is actually one of great distance.

To sum up this examination of "The Battle of Brunanburh," we may say that this speaker, although addressing us in the third person, is very much in evidence. He is known to us, and to his intended readership, as a chronicler, a scholar in government service, as it were, and thus a man with two major interests: the preservation of history, and the well-being of the kingdom in which he gains his livelihood. The poet, of course, must have been a far more complex person: as a cleric, his service to God must have been a major influence on his outlook, but here he presents himself, in the person of his speaker, as chronicler only. Any ideas he may have had on the victory of the Christians over the heathens are irrelevant to his topic. One might consider his peculiar point of view a liability in writing about a military expedition, but we find, on the contrary, that he has used these limitations to advantage. His ignorance of the particulars of the battle becomes omniscience in his speaker, and his spatial distance from Brunanburh has given him the larger perspective that imparts credibility to this poem. His limitations of space and time have been put to work to condense both space and time into the field outside Brunanburh on the day of the battle. Having adopted the nonpersonal voice out of necessity, he has used his powers of invention to create a speaker who is perhaps the perfect voice for the topic, the context, and the emotion of the poem.

"The Ruin" is assuredly the most successful of the extant Old English lyrics using the non-personal voice, and it is most difficult of these to examine, not only because a large hole in the folios on which it is written has deprived us of many lines, but also because there are no clues, either external or internal, to the speaker's identity, or even to what relationship he might have been thought to bear to his topic, although his wonder is clear to any reader. For us, reading is further troubled by modern scholarship which usually presents "The Ruin" as either an elegy manqué or an inexpert Dark Ages travelogue. The method is first to posit "The Ruin" as an elegy and then to fault it as too impersonal, or to posit it as a realistic description of some actual ruin, usually Bath, and then to fault it as too inaccurate to be a successful bit of realistic description. As explained in the first chapter, the concept of the elegy as a poetic genre is not particularly helpful in reading any of the so-called elegies.[10] As for attempts to identify a particular site, this practice assumes the modern concept of realism, and it leads one into going at "The Ruin" with a shovel as though it were an archeological dig rather than a lyric poem. The siting of "The Ruin" is further troubled by the way it limits the date of composition. The ruins of Bath were not visible after the mid-eighth century, and by the late tenth century, when the Exeter Book was compiled, the Roman floors were some eight feet below the surface, which facts are usually taken to indicate that the poem was composed in the seventh or early eighth century. If the poem is in fact this early, the Exeter Book anthologist must have decided to include in his collection a two- or three-hundred-year-old poem, the setting of which was surely obscure to him and his readership. If one accepts this possibility, one might argue that the anthologist included it for some allegorical value known to, or presumed by, him, whether or not he was aware of its historical background, and the poem has in fact been read recently as an allegory of human anatomy or of the Babylon of Revelation. We simply do not know whether the ruin of the poem refers to an actuality or is an imaginative construction, but clearly its poet was sufficiently competent either to have imagined or to have mentally recreated the site in the tenth century, whether or not he used historical records of seventh- or eighth-century Bath or first-hand information on some tenth-century ruin such as Hadrian's Wall.[11]

I begin this examination of the speaker's voice, then, with the poem itself, setting aside all questions of allegory, realism, and genre. The speaker's point of view is far different from that of the speaker of "Brunanburh," for the speaker of "The Ruin" is clearly *in situ*. The first verse of the poem is "Wrætlic is þes wealstan": this wall stone is ornamental, and it is wondrous, or curious, since *wrætlic* denotes both the concepts of "decorated" and "wondrous." Such an opening places the speaker directly on the spot; it is not *a* wall stone, or even *the* wall stone, but *this* wall stone, the one right here in my hands, he seems to say. Lines 3–6a then give quick visual glimpses of several different spots:

> Hrofas sind gehrorene,   hreorge torras,
> hrungeat berofen,   hrim on lime,
> scearde scurbeorge   scorene, gedrorene,
> ældo undereotone.

[Roofs are fallen, towers are in ruins, the barred gate is despoiled, frost is on the mortar, the shower-shelter (i.e., roof) is mutilated, shorn down, fallen, undermined by age.]

The reader has the sense in these lines that the speaker has looked up from the wall stone he has been examining to see the roofs, towers, and gates. He is close enough to all these to see frost on the mortar, and to describe the wall as "ræghar ond readfah" [lichen-old, and red in color, 10a]. The poem conveys a sense of a static speaker, standing or sitting at some spot next to the wall within the ruin, not wandering through it.[12] The speaker is as static, then, physically, as his topic. There does seem to be a great deal of vertical movement in the poem, with many words denoting the towering and the lofty, and many descriptions of falling motion (Calder "Perspective"), but this movement is entirely in the mind of the speaker as he recreates the vertical structures and then, with his mind's eye, watches them fall.

The sense of movement in the poem comes not from movement through space, but through time, and it is this aspect that demonstrates the speaker's control over his material, however much he seems to be held thrall to the wonder of the ruin. His mind wanders first from the present moment to the eschatological future: "oþ hund cnea werþeoda gewitan" [until a hundred generations of men pass, 8b–9a].[13] Then, in verse 9b, the tense and the speaker's thoughts shift to the past: "Oft þæs wag gebad ræghar ond readfah rice æfter oþrum, ofstonden under stormum" [Often this wall, lichen-old and red-colored, endured, kingdom after kingdom, remaining under storms]. After a hiatus of several illegible lines, we find the speaker now in the more distant past, the time of prosperity in the city, as he describes in lines 19–23 the building of the city and the joyous sounds of men in the meadhall. Line 24 marks an abrupt shift to the nearer past, the time of the destruction of the city, as the speaker describes in lines 24–29a the deaths of the inhabitants by pestilence. In 29b, the speaker is just as abruptly back in the present, explaining that this is why the city is now in ruin. In 32b he is again in the prosperous past in which men gazed on the treasure of the city and the wall enclosed the hot baths in its center. Here we must stop, as the text again becomes mostly illegible. The pattern that develops in tracing the time sequence of the speaker's thoughts is one of back and forth movement among a range of points in time. Time is fluid for the speaker, but the movement through time is not random or disordered, for the prosperous past of the city tugs on the speaker and finally becomes more important to him than the prospect of the ruin. Time provides the structure of the poem, and time ultimately provides the topic. The reader experiences the speaker's emotions as they unfold from his initial wonder at the ornamented wall stone, through his thoughts on the future of the site, and throughout the recreation of the past. What is remarkable about the poet's use of time is the contrast between the plastic time of the poem and the static and inflexible nature of the ruin and of the speaker's physical presence in it. The silent ruin throbs with the ebb and flow of time. It is in this way that the speaker's mind comes to dominate the poem and its subject.[14]

As mentioned above, it is common to find the so-called impersonal tone of the speaker emphasized in modern criticism of the poem.[15] These critics are right in thinking that the speaker makes few personal comments and expresses no personal grief, but the reader who has engaged with the speaker's evolving wonder throughout the poem finds that personal intrusion from the speaker is unnecessary. The speaker has succeeded in communicating to us his wonder at the forces of time and his ability imaginatively to counteract those forces. As one critic so aptly puts it, "it is a very identifiable persona who addresses the reader" (Fanagan 293). That the poet has succeeded in this poem, that, in the words of Derek Pearsall, it is "among the most enduringly beautiful poems in English" (51) should tell us something about the effectiveness of the nonpersonal speaker.

This chapter has taken us from a relatively simple lyric, "Cædmon's Hymn," about which we have a great deal of information on the poet and his purposes, to a relatively sophisticated lyric, "The Ruin," about which we have no information on the poet and little on the contemporary context of the poem. One remaining nonpersonal lyric, "The Father's Lament," has been reserved for last because its epic context and multiple layers of speakers demand a somewhat different approach than that taken with the independent lyrics.

"The Father's Lament" is one of two lyrics embedded in the narrative of *Beowulf,* both of which occur within two hundred lines of one another near the beginning of the third section—that is, after a hiatus of more than fifty years in the narrative. This section of the poem is extremely digressive, even by the norm of the *Beowulf* poet, and thus contains in a short space many of the thematic and narrative strands of the epic, most notably, regicide, parricide, the futility of vengeance, and ethnic extinction. The lyric itself is embedded in Beowulf's speech to his retainers on the ness before the dragon's cave. This speech seems to most modern readers to be awkwardly placed, interrupting the narration of the dragon fight for the achronological insertion of Beowulf's family history. Furthermore, much of the information given in the speech seems incongruous to the narrative context, and the subject of the lyric incongruous to the speech. However, by focussing on the speaker rather than the speech, one discovers that the lyric provides the psychological bridge needed to integrate the entire digression, if one may call it that, into the context of the frame narrative.

The speech may be summarized as follows. Beowulf tells us first that his eldest foster brother and cousin, Herebeald, was killed in a hunting accident by Herebeald's brother Hathcyn. Next, their father, Beowulf's uncle and foster father Hrethel, died, presumably of grief over this tragedy. Third, Hathcyn was himself killed in a battle against the Swedes. The lyric is inserted directly after the recollection of the accidental fratricide of Herebeald by Hathcyn. Beowulf's comment on this death is, "Þæt wæs feohleās gefeoht, fyrenum gesyngad, hreðre hygemeðe" [that was a fight not to be atoned for with money, a crime done in sin, wearying to the heart, 2441–42a]. In other words, the troubling aspect of this death is that the victim's family cannot claim compensation as a way to expiate their grief, since this family is identical with the family of the slayer. Although an unavengeable death like this was probably not a unique situation, it could not have happened all that frequently; thus, Beowulf provides his audience with a simile to explain Hreðel's situation. This simile is the lyric poem under discussion here:

> Swā bið geōmorlīc gomelum ceorle
> tō gebīdanne, þæt his byre rīde
> giong on galgan; þonne hē gyd wrece,
> sārigne sang, þonne his sunu hangað
> hrefne tō hrōðre, ond hē him helpe ne mæg
> eald ond infrōd ænige gefremman.
> Symble bið gemyndgad morna gehwylce
> eaforan ellorsīð; ōðres ne gȳmeð
> tō gebīdanne burgum in innan
> yrfeweardas, þonne se ān hafað

þurh dēaðes nȳd   dǣda gefondad.
Gesyhð sorhcearig   on his suna būre
wīnsele wēstne,   windge reste
rēote berofene,——   rīdend swefað,
hæleð in hoðman;   nis þǣr hearpan swēg,
gomen in geardum,   swylce ðǣr iū wǣron.
xxxv Gewīteð þonne on sealman,   sorhlēoð gæleð
ān æfter ānum;   þūhte him eall tō rūm,
wongas ond wīcstede.[16]   (2444–62)

[Thus it is sad for an old man to endure that his son should swing young on the gallows. Then he might compose a lay, a sorrowful song, when his son hangs as a joy for the raven, and he, old and very wise, is not able to give him any help. He is always reminded, every morning, of his heir's departure; he does not care to await another inside the homestead when the one has experienced deeds through death's compulsion. He gazes sorrowfully on his son's dwelling—a deserted winehall, a windswept couch robbed of its joy. The horsemen and heroes sleep in their graves. There is no sound of the harp, no game in the yard as there once were. He retires then to his bed and sings a sorrowful song for his son. The fields and the dwellings seemed to him all too spacious.]

Thus, it looks as if Beowulf's thoughts have strayed far indeed from his own immanent death. He had begun with his first association with the royal family, proceeded to recount a royal death, ranged out into the theme of parricide, then that of the impossibility of expiation, and finally finds himself discussing a fictive execution and the extinction of a fictive family line. It is little wonder that readers often feel that the narrative is awkwardly held up here: Geatish royal history has little to do with the dragon fight, and the fictive execution has little to do with Geatish royal history. And yet the lyric's subject does have something to do with its speaker, Beowulf.

The first thing that readers usually notice about this poem is the unlooked-for appearance of the deserted mead hall and the associated images of the warriors and the harp. One asks oneself why the hanged man's court should be deserted and his retainers dead. A common explanation is that grief over a death suggests this cluster of images for the Anglo-Saxons, whether or not they are appropriate to the narrative background. Charles W. Kennedy writes, "These lines suggest how readily the characteristic images of elegiac invention hardened into a conventional pattern. The evidence is found in the fact that in this passage certain of these characteristic elegiac images are employed in circumstances in which there is no grounding of realism to suggest them" (*Earliest* 129).

Kennedy is certainly correct in finding that there is no "grounding of realism" in this lyric, but this is not necessarily evidence that these elements have been used only because they are conventional. Klaeber is closer to the mark: "The explanation is that the old man falls into a reverie, seeing with his mind's eye the scene of desolation, or, in other words, the poet passes from the actual, specific situation to a typical motive of elegiac poetry" (*Beowulf* 213–14). However, the specific situation of the execution is not "actual," for the entire lyric is a reverie, Beowulf's reverie. When we consider the epic context, we see that Beowulf's mind must surely be on his own death and on the fatal consequences of his death to the Geatish people. It is his own mead hall, not the hanged man's or Herebeald's, that is deserted and windswept—in fact, burnt to the ground by the dragon's wrath. The sound of the harp and the games in the yard are no more because it is Beowulf's own horsemen and heroes who sleep in their graves: the dragon did not spare "āht cwices" [any of the living, 2314]. The speaker's mind is thus effectively represented by this lyric, albeit in a narratively round-about fashion, as Beowulf imposes some details of his own projected death onto two stories, one historical and one fictional, in which they make little literal sense. A second incongruity between the lyric and its narrative setting, briefly noted above, becomes clear when one looks at the poem through the speaker. Hrethel does have an heir after Herebeald's death—in fact he has three, his two younger sons and his sister's son, Beowulf—while the hanged man's father, like Beowulf, has none. Beowulf has here conflated two persons into the subject of the lyric: the old man is like Hrethel, in that his son is dead and unavengeable, and he is like Beowulf, in that he has no heir. The hanged man himself is like Beowulf in that his court is desolate and his men dead. Third, the one point at which the lyric and the contextual speech do touch—the theme of the impossibility of vengeance—is just as relevant to Beowulf's situation, for the dragon is no more likely than Grendel to pay compensation.

The lyric thus performs two functions: it reveals Beowulf's state of mind, and it foreshadows the ending of the epic, introducing the reader to the horror to come. Read in this way, the lyric is no longer conventional, but an emotionally charged cluster that moves the reader into identifying with Beowulf's emotions, as well as into the mood of this final section of the epic.

That this lyric should be so moving is even more remarkable when one looks at the narrative distance between the reader and the events of the lyric. First, the reader is in the hands of the narrator who is relating a story that includes Beowulf's speech. Second, Beowulf's speech is a narrative of a part of the past not included in the frame narrative. Third, in this narrative within a narrative, Beowulf examines the emotions of a man, Hrethel, who is not a character in the frame narrative, and whose emotions he can only guess at, having been a child at the time of these events. Fourth, these emotions are projected onto a fictive character in a simileic aside, which is also a lyric poem. But there is a further layer: the old man of the lyric is said to compose a "sorrowful song" (2446b–47a). Lines 2450–59 have all the signs of being the song composed by the old man, and it is in these lines that the so-called conventional elements of the deserted mead hall appear. These lines remain in the third person as indirect discourse rather than changing to the first-person voice of the old man; Beowulf says that the old man sings that he is reminded every morning of his son's death, and so on. The lines immediately following this pro-posed song within a song reiterate, in Beowulf's words, that the old man sings his song alone on his couch, and that the song was prompted by his *feeling* that the house and fields were empty, which is precisely the theme of the deserted mead hall in the lines pro-posed as his song. This lyric is structurally at an astonishing remove from the epic narrator—the only comparable instances of such layering of speakers in Old English poetry are "The Dream of the Rood" and "The Wanderer." The poet of *Beowulf* has taken a large risk in straying so far away from the story of the dragon, but only narratively speaking. In fact, this multilayering of speakers is emi-nently successful in this lyric, and in the epic, for it effectively involves the reader in the emotion of the tragedy to come.

This discussion of poems using the non-personal voice has dem-onstrated just how successful this voice can be in a lyric poem. Caedmon, the chronicler-poet who composed "Brunanburh," and the author of "The Ruin" all remove themselves from their works. Caedmon's speaker omits himself from his hymn so that he can speak in a universal voice; the chronicler's speaker reveals himself as an outsider to his martial topic in order to establish himself as an authority on its wider significance, and the author of "The Ruin" rejects the possibilities of a first-person speaker in order to achieve for the reader an even greater immediacy of his response. In each of these poems, the reader is put in direct touch with the content of the poem, with little or no obstacle in the way of a personality with whom he must develop some sympathy. The case of "The Father's Lament" is somewhat different: the *Beowulf* poet chose multiple layers of speakers, personalities, and time for reasons that have to do with his purposes in the epic, for taken out of context, this third-person lyric is only moderately successful. The outcome of this study, then, is the suggestion that "nonpersonal" need not imply "impersonal" but, in the hands of a capable poet, the nonpersonal voice can be an effective vehicle for the communication of a wide range of emotional responses to a wide range of topics.

5

The Fictive Speaker

The group of poems that use a fictive speaker—that is, a speaker who is a fictitious human character and who appears in the poems as an "I"—is far more homogeneous than the groups of poems using inanimate, adoptable, or nonpersonal speakers. The six poems using fictive speakers—"The Seafarer," "Deor," "The Wife's Lament," "Wulf and Eadwacer," "The Riming Poem," and the fragment "Resignation"—are all found uniquely in the Exeter Book, and are very much alike in structure, tone, and topic. For one thing, all the fictive speakers but Deor are alone and seem for the most part to be unaware of their audiences, although the seafarer and the king in "The Riming Poem" do indicate at the end of their poems that they are aware of an audience or readership by closing with *uton* "let us" constructions (further discussed below). These lyrics are thus best thought of as soliloquies, internal monologues intended to be overheard by the reader. Deor differs from the other five speakers in that he is clearly addressing an audience, like the speakers of the *Chronicle* poems and manuscript prefaces, but while the chroniclers and personified manuscripts address an audience of readers, Deor addresses an audience of listeners. Deor is a *scop* and he addresses a group of people assembled to hear him perform.

The fictive speakers also have in common the anacoluthic use of person, a device that we modern readers often find confusing. The text of each of the poems alternates between first and third person or, in the case of "Wulf," among first person singular, dual, and plural, in a manner that seems to the modern reader illogical, or insufficiently motivated. The implications of this sort of anacoluthon must be faced in each poem individually, but it is probably safe to say at the outset that a less rigid use of person was common to these poems and that therefore one ought not to make too much of it—one certainly ought not to assign lines to various speakers on the basis of personal pronouns.[1]

Another feature that distinguishes the fictive speaker is a far greater use of nature imagery, especially personification and the pathetic fallacy, than is found in any of the lyrics outside this group. Even in the brief fictive lyric "The Last Survivor" (*Beowulf* 2247–66), personification much like that found in the independent lyrics plays a major role, first in the apostrophe to earth—"Heald þū nū, hrūse" [Hold now, earth, 2247a]—and then in the animation of the byrnie:

> gē swylce sēo herepād,   sīo æt hilde gebād
> ofer borda gebræc   bite īrena,
> brosnað æfter beorne.   Ne mæg byrnan hring
> æfter wīgfruman   wīde fēran,
> hæleðum be healfe.

(*Beowulf* 2258–62a)

[and the coat of mail, which endured the bite of iron swords over the breaking of shields in battle, decays after the warrior. The byrnie cannot fare far after the war-chief, by the side of the hero.]

The best known example of the pathetic fallacy in the fictive lyrics is the passage from "Wulf" in which the speaker weeps while it rains, but similar images are found, and play a major role, in each of the other poems except the fragment "Resignation." It seems that that since the fictive speaker of these poems must be given a character in 120 lines or fewer without recourse to dialogue (which is found only in didactic poems), the poet has called on the natural setting to fill in the mood he wishes to convey. However, Alvin A. Lee, in his seminal study of the Christian mythological background of the Old English poetic corpus, *The Guest-Hall of Eden,* has discussed this feature at length, not only as found in the lyrics, but in the narratives and such short poems as "The Seasons for Fasting" and "The Order of theWorld," stating that "the Old English poetic uses of images of the cycles of nature is a major symbolic device for giving a sense of movement and order to the poetry" (130). It is nevertheless true that such nature imagery is largely absent from lyric poems using other kinds of speakers, "The Ruin" and "The Wanderer" being the most salient exceptions.

The most important respect in which these six poems are similar, however, is what I would like to call their homiletic structure. Each poem expends most of its energies on presenting a character and situation that will engage the reader, and then ends with a bit of wisdom that is proven true by the lyric utterance that precedes it. "Deor" differs from the other five poems in that it employs this pattern not once but six times: the speaker presents six *exempla* and follows each by the same one-line proverb. This pattern is nearly unique to the fictive speaker, although it also appears in "The Wanderer" and, in a modified form, in the "The Dream of the Rood." In each poem, the fictive speaker illustrates the gnomic conclusion: far from having the flavor of endings tacked onto the lyrics by later redactors, each aphorism carries the germ of the lyric, the reason for its existence. Two of the poems end with wisdom that is not simply stated but rather urged upon the reader: "The Seafarer" and "The Riming Poem" are thus hortatory and more truly homiletic than the other four. They are also the only two that deal with explicitly Christian themes. The two hortatory lyrics, furthermore, each employ a speaker who is what Rosemary Woolf has called a "representative type" ("*Wanderer*" 192). The seafarer and the king of "The Riming Poem" are not only type characters, but also metaphors. The other four fictive speakers, on the other hand, who present gnomic rather than hortatory wisdom, are what Woolf would call "individual" characters, and these function on a strictly literal level.

Of the four poems that use an individual fictive speaker, one, "Resignation," is assuredly a fragment, and the other three, "Wulf and Eadwacer," "The Wife's Lament," and "Deor," are perhaps the most puzzling poems in the language. In chapter 3, I considered the integrity of "Resignation" in light of the scholarship of Alan Bliss and Allen J. Frantzen, who argue that our received text is actually the beginning of one poem and the end of another, conflated by the loss of a leaf in the Exeter Book manuscript. In that chapter, I considered the first 68 lines of the *ASPR* text, which constitute the beginning of a prayer, under the title "The Penitent's Prayer" and have now to take up the remaining fragment, which Bliss and Frantzen designate an ethopoeic narrative. Whether the complete poem was a narrative is impossible to tell, but the fragment we have is lyrical. Bliss and Frantzen's title for this fragment, "Resignation B," is not a happy one, as they admit: for convenience sake, I refer to this fragment as "Resignation," and use the *ASPR* line numbers. Thus, the lines of the fragment are numbered 69 through 118.

Beginning at line 69, then, the speaker tells us that he wishes to laugh and to trust himself and to set out on the journey he must make (69–75). He believes he inadvertently must have angered God, who is apparently punishing him with hardships that grow greater each year (76–88a). This is the reason that he prepares to depart from his homeland (88b–89a). The solitary exile (referred to

in the third person), with whom God is wroth, is always miserable
(89b-96a)—the speaker seems to be projecting his future here.
Unfortunately, the speaker is too poor to make the journey (96b–
104). Then, addressing God, he admits to being "mode [s]eoc" [sick
at heart, 109b], unable to love any one or to continue his life (105–
116). However, he concludes:

> Giet biþ þæt selast,   þonne mon him sylf ne mæg
> wyrd onwendan,   þæt he þonne wel þolige.

(117–18)

[Yet, when a man cannot change for himself what is to be, then it is best
that he suffer well]

One striking point in this fragment is the concreteness of the
ocean voyage by which the speaker desires to escape his present
troubles but which he will not be able to afford: "hwy ic gebycge
bat on sæwe, fleot on faroðe" [by what means I might buy a boat on
the sea, a vessel on the shore, 100–101a]. This journey is surely to
be understood only as an actual physical journey: there is nothing
about it to suggest the symbol, metaphor, or allegory as there is
about the sea voyages in "The Wanderer" and "The Seafarer."

A second striking feature is the concreteness in the character of
the speaker. The fragment is rife with details about a personality
not found (to my knowledge) elsewhere among Anglo-Saxon literary speakers. This speaker places his trust in himself (71b) rather
than in God. He avoids taking responsibility for his sins: "Huru me
frea witeð sume þara synna þe ic me sylf ne conn ongietan
gleawlice" [Indeed, the Lord blames me for some sins that I
myself cannot diligently perceive, 76b–77a]. He blames others for
his troubles: "me wæs a cearu symle lufena to leane" [sorrow was
always my reward for love, 115b–116a]. Indeed, in one passage
(which I read ironically—no doubt anachronistically), he blames
even God for his suffering: "ic a þolade geara gehwylce (gode ealles
þonc!) modearfoþa ma þonne on oþrum" [each year I always suffer
(thanks to God for all!) more mental anguish than the last, 85b–87].
In the words of Bliss and Frantzen, he is "the kind of man who
never succeeds in any of his enterprises, and who blames everyone
but himself for his failures" (397). Although he admits that God will
be able to remedy his troubles after death, he seems oddly unaware
that he ought to be seeking God's mercy in the meanwhile. He is, in
short, impious. If he were not clearly a Christian speaker, he would

not be so puzzling. The gnomic conclusion, quoted above, is of a piece with this impious speaker: "when a man himself cannot change his fate," he had just better suffer rather than seek God's mercy as Christian sinners ought to do.

Although the beginning of the poem (perhaps as much as two pages worth, or some 60 lines, since the preceding "Penitent's Prayer" seems nearly complete) is lost to us, it is clear that we have here a male speaker who is a highly individualized character and whose situation illustrates a non-Christian gnome that concludes the poem. The peevish speaker discourses sourly with himself, rehearsing his trials for a reader he does not acknowledge, but who, oddly enough, is quite likely to identify strongly with his emotions. All of us have days when we feel like this.

There is little more to say about the poem: it is extremely diffuse and nearly devoid of metaphor. There is only the one mention of the growing forest carrying its branches and awaiting its fate (105–6a), which serves as a contrast to the speaker's lack of purpose and nonintegration of character, but the fragment demonstrates nothing of the dense imagery that illuminates the speakers of "Wulf" and "The Wife's Lament."

It is this highly condensed quality of "Wulf and Eadwacer" that probably accounts for much of its obscurity, although one sometimes feels that much of the poem's puzzlement derives from the scholarship surrounding it, which leaves us, as one critic writes, "dismayed at the amount of ingenuity expended on its interpretation, and the triviality of the results gained" (Whitbread 150).[2] Nevertheless, the text as we have it is quite obscure. The speaker allots few words to her own situation, a matter of paramount importance for the other speakers of this type, at least in the first sections of their utterances. Here, on the contrary, the greatest part of the 19 lines is given over to a discussion of her men and son. The beginning of the poem is very abrupt, contrasting with the careful and formal openings of "The Riming Poem," "The Seafarer," and "The Wife's Lament," and with the beginning of the wanderer's utterance in line 8 of that poem and of Deor's first-person utterance in line 35 of his lyric. Without attempting to force "Wulf" into a mold defined by these other poems, I do think it sensible to allow for the possibility that there are some lines missing from the beginning of the poem, the spot in which the other fictive speakers concentrate first-person singular pronouns and personal details. In support of this conjecture is the odd fact that the speaker does not reveal her sex (with a feminine inflectional ending) until line 10, more than half-way through the poem, a circumstance which must have made comprehension difficult on the first reading or hearing if the text is indeed complete as we have it.[3]

We can say for certain that the speaker is a woman, that she is separated from someone named Wulf, for whom she longs and weeps, that she has an ambiguous sexual relationship with a man referred to as "se beaducafa" [the one bold in battle, 11a], and that she addresses someone named Eadwacer, who is probably "se beaducafa." Whatever the situation may be, the speaker's emotional response to it is clear enough. In an apostrophe to Wulf she exclaims:

> Wulf, min Wulf,   wena me þine
> seoce gedydon,   þine seldcymas
> murnende mod,   nales meteliste.

> (13–15)

[Wulf, my Wulf, hopes of you have made me sick, your rare visits, a troubled mind, not lack of food.]

The speaker is not only pining for reunion with Wulf, but is sick with worry for him as well. Her weeping for Wulf is echoed by the weather—"þonne hit wæs renig weder ond ic reotugu sæt" [when it was rainy weather and I sat weeping, 10]—and her separation from him is echoed by the islands they live on. His is "fæst" and "fenne biworpen" [fast and surrounded by a fen, 5]—thus it is he who is enclosed and shut off, not she, as some critics think. In short, the pathetic fallacy is well employed to demonstrate to the reader just how isolated and grief stricken the speaker is.

As for her feelings for Eadwacer, whom I take to be "se beaducafa," she says:

> þonne mec se baducafa   bogum bilegde
> wæs me wyn to þon,   wæs me hwæþre eac lað,

> (11–12)

[when the one bond in battle enfolded me with his arms, it was a joy to me, to a point, but was also hateful to me]

which is clear enough. A few lines later she addresses him in an apostrophe:

Gehyrest þu, Eadwacer?   Uncerne earne hwelp
bireð wulf to wuda.

(16–17)

[Do you hear, Eadwacer? Wulf bears our (?) whelp to the woods.]

These lines are certainly obscure. *hwelp* "whelp" must be a meta-phor for "child," perhaps prompted by Wulf's name, but *earne* is a *hapax legomena* whose meaning is unknown. The *ASPR* further confuses the matter by leaving *wulf* in the lower case, as though the child had been dragged off by a wolf rather than borne away by Wulf, as is more likely. This apostrophe is so brief that it is difficult to be sure of the speaker's tone here, but taken together with her earlier comments on both men, the lines sound bitter and defiant as she taunts Eadwacer with Wulf's possession of the former's son. Nevertheless, this means that the speaker herself is deprived of her son, too, as well as of her lover.

Although we cannot know for certain what the speaker's situation is, or what all these details add up to, there are plenty of details (at least about her familial relationships) and her situation as she describes it could hardly have been typical. The only general state-ment in the entire poem is the conclusion:

Þæt mon eaþe tosliteð   þætte næfre gesomnad wæs,
uncer giedd geador.

(18–19)

[Man can easily put asunder that which was never joined—our story together.]

These lines are a direct allusion to and inversion of Matthew 19:6, which reads, in the Vulgate version: "Quod ergo Deus conjunxit, homo non separaret." (My translation above deliberately echoes the English Authorized Version.)[4] Clearly, the poem has illustrated the gnomic statement that an unsanctified marriage is easily de-stroyed by human agency, whether it is Eadwacer who has sun-dered her illicit union with Wulf or Wulf who, she hopes, will sunder her illicit union with Eadwacer. The latter reading is sup-ported by Wulf's abduction of the boy, who is the fruit and the exemplification of her union with Eadwacer, but perhaps the apho-rism comments on both relationships. That our text is probably a fragment makes it difficult to say. In any case, when taken on its own the aphorism is not likely to move any reader the way it does when it comes at the end of this poem. Having empathized with the speaker's fear, grief, worry, and sexual frustration, all of which are caused by her somehow having become involved with two men at the same time, the reader is quite willing to acknowledge the proverb's truth.

"The Wife's Lament" concerns a similar situation, expresses similar emotions, and presents modern readers with similar difficulties. The speaker begins with a careful statement of purpose:

> Ic þis giedd wrece   bi me ful geomorre,
> minre sylfre sið.   Ic þæt secgan mæg,
> hwæt ic yrmþa gebad,   siþþan ic up weox,
> niwes oþþe ealdes,   no ma þonne nu.
> A ic wite wonn   minra wræcsiþa.

[I utter this song (or account) about my very sad self, my own journey. I can tell what hardships I endured since I grew up, recently or long ago, no more than now. I always suffered the torment of my miseries (or persecutions or exiles.)]

The speaker identifies herself immediately as a woman by the feminine inflections in lines 1 and 2, and she is quite specific in stating what she proposes to tell. She goes on to relate the particulars in lines 6–28, which present some problems in chronology for the modern reader trying to put all this in tidy order. To summarize: "Ærest" [First] my lord departed; I worried about his whereabouts (6–8). "Ða" [Then/next/at that time] I departed "folgað secan" [to seek a retinue or service in a retinue, 9b]. The man's kinsman began (simple preterite) to plot to separate us (11–14). My (cruel) lord bade me take up residence (here/in a grove) where I have no friends (15–17a).[5] "Forþon" (connecting ths to either the preceding or the following) my mind is sad (17b). "Ða" [Then/next/ at that time] I found a man well suited to me, unfortunate, sad, and thinking of death (18–20). We two often vowed that nothing but death would part us; afterwards that changed. Now our love is as if it never were. I must suffer a state of feud with, or because of, my beloved (21–26). I was ordered to dwell in an "eorðscræf" [cave, underground dwelling], under an oak tree, in a grove (27–28).

If these events are understood to have occurred in the order given, then we must take it that the kinsmen plotted to separate the speaker from her husband after they were already separated, that

the speaker's voluntary departure was followed by two banish-
ments, that she became involved with a second man only after her
banishment by her husband, and so on, which is difficult to understand. Most readers understand the speaker to be the loyal wife of a
sympathetic nobleman who was forced to abandon her because he
died, was outlawed, or feared that he would become the next victim
of a feud, although some have seen him as hostile to the speaker.[6]
None of these readings is without problems. The hostile-husband
reading is contradicted by the speaker's apparent affection for him
and furthermore requires the introduction of some motivation for
his hostility (such as adultery on her part), while the sympathetic-
husband reading requires the introduction of some criminal activity
on his part, unless we can justify the meaning of "Ærest min
hlaford gewat heonan of leodum ofer yþa gelac" [first my lord
departed hence from the nation over the tossing of waves, 6–7a] as
"First my lord died," which, although possible, is unlikely in light
of the next clause: "hæfde ic uhtceare hwær min leodfruma londes
wære" [I had anxiety in the hours before dawn about where in the
land my prince might be, 7b–8]. Further troubling to the modern
reader is how the speaker could live in this isolated setting.[7]

This section is longer and more detailed than the corresponding
sections of any of the other fictive poems. The speakers of "The
Riming Poem," "The Seafarer," and "Wulf" make no mention of
the train of events that led to their current circumstances (although
in the latter, this information may well have been lost from the text).
However, this section in "The Wife's Lament," obscure as it is, is
clearly very particular, and its relatively great length must be necessary either to identify the speaker as a character already known to
the reader from epic or folklore material,[8] or to provide the reader
with enough of her background so that he can understand how an
unnamed person could have found herself in such an unusual situation. The fact that this section means little to modern readers need
indicate only that we are not the poet's intended readership, and
thus does not necessarily point toward an allegorical reading,[9] or to
the conclusion that the poet was being purposely vague in order the
better to create her mood.

With the last sentence of the background section (that is, beginning on line 27), however, we can begin to discuss mood, as the
speaker moves into the present, and the descriptive section of her
utterance. She was ordered *wunian* "to dwell, exist" within a grove
of trees, under an oak tree, in the (N.B. the definite article) earth-
cave. As is often pointed out, the grove of trees containing an oak
probably means that the spot is a heathen place of worship; the

eorðscræf, however, is not typically associated with such a place, and thus may be taken as a further particular, whether it means "cave" or "grave." The next sentence, beginning the description proper, contains the disturbing paratactic construction that presents the speaker's state of mind as one of several descriptive statements concerning her surroundings:

> Eald is þes eorðsele,   eal ic eom oflongad,
> sindon dena dimme,   duna uphea,
> bitre burgtunas,   brerum beweaxne,
> wic wynna leas.

(29–32a)

[This earth-hall is old, I am altogether seized with longing, the valleys are dim, the hills high, the walled towns bitter, grown over with briars, the village without joys]

Here, the pathetic fallacy is created by making the speaker's longing grammatically parallel with the age, darkness, enclosing nature, and joylessness of her surroundings. Darkness was introduced earlier, at the beginning of her account of her history, in the word *uhtcearu* "worry in the hours before dawn" (7b), and this darkest hour is reintroduced here:

> Frynd sind on eorþan,
> leofe lifgende,   leger weardiað,
> þonne ic on uhtan   ana gonge
> under actreo   geond þas eorðscrafu.

(33b–36)

[Lovers, living loved ones, are on earth, sleeping in their beds, when I alone before dawn wander under the oak tree, throughout the earth-caves.]

The lines immediately following contain a jarring image of summer and light, which contrast sharply with the situation described:

> Þær ic sittan mot   sumorlangne dæg,
> þær ic wepan mæg   mine wræcsiþas,

(37–38)

[There (i.e., under the oak tree and among the earthcaves, or in the earthcaves) I may sit for a summer-long day, there I can weep for my miseries (or exiles).]

The expression "sumorlangne dæg" apparently means "for the space of time as long as a day in the summer," that is, "a long time," but the image of daylight and summertime contrasts with and thus underscores the darkness in which the speaker sits, positioned as she is in the shadows.

This passage is the emotional center of the poem, framed on the one end by the narrative background (6–26) and on the other by the gnomic conclusion (42–53). In this entire passage, the speaker conveys her emotion chiefly by means of the pathetic fallacy. She has told us that she is miserable and has given us the reasons for her misery in her separation from the man she loves, but we do not really begin to empathize with her until this passage, which parallels her emotions with her physical surroundings: both are dark, confined, and solitary.

The concluding section, lines 42ff, falls in the proper place for a gnomic conclusion, and that is how most critics would now read it.[10] This section begins with a problematic sentence in the subjective mood:

> A scyle geong mon   wesan geomormod,
> heard heortan geþoht,   swylce habban sceal
> bliþe gebæro,   eac þon breostceare,
> sinsorgna gedreag,   sy æt him sylfum gelong
> eal his worulde wyn,   sy ful wide fah
> feorres folclondes

$$(42–47a)$$

[A young person must always be sad-minded, his heart's thought hard; he must have a blithe bearing just as he has the anxiety of his heart, a throng of constant sorrows. All his joy in the world may be dependent upon himself; he may be very widely banished, far from his country.]

The word *monn* can be used of a person of either sex, making it possible that the speaker applies this aphorism to her own experience, although this is of course possible even if the aphorism refers to male experience. However, the content of the gnomic statement echoes the situation not of the speaker, but of the man "me full gemæcne" [very well suited to me, 18a], described in lines 19–20 as

> heardsæligne,   hygegeomorne,
> mod miþendne,   morþor hycgendne

[unfortunate, sad in thought, concealing his mind, thinking of death],

who yet makes a vow "[b]liþe gebæro" [with a blithe bearing, 21a].
The gnomic lines quoted above (42–47a), therefore, are illustrated
by the situation of the speaker's lord. To these gnomic lines are
appended more particulars about the man's situation:

> . . . þæt min freond siteð
> under stanhliþe   storme behrimed,
> wine werigmod,   wæter beflowen
> on dreorsele.

(47b–50a)

[. . . so that my lover sits under a stone cliff, frosted by a storm, my
weary minded friend, surrounded by water in a dreary hall.]

Here it is the lover whose situation is echoed by his physical
surroundings—in this case, imagined physical surroundings.
Whether these lines allude to the icy Germanic hell, or to the lord's
drowning (Rissanen 98), or to some other recognizable setting, they
clearly suggest the physical surroundings of the winter seashore
that we find connected with the mental states of both the wanderer
and the seafarer.
    The concluding sentence of the poem is a second aphorism:

> Wa bið þam þe sceal
> of langoþe   leofes abidan.

(52b–53)

[There is woe for him who must await his loved one with longing.]

This aphorism clearly applies to the speaker, who has already used
forms of the word *langian* three other times in reference to herself
(14b, 29b, and 41a). This second aphorism is illustrated by the
speaker's own story.
    Thus, "The Wife's Lament" comprises two gnomic statements,
the first to the effect that young people will have trouble under any
circumstances and that they had best put a good countenance on it,
and the second, that a person who has to wait for her loved one's

return has nothing but grief. Both these aphorisms are illustrated by the wife separated from her trouble-plagued husband. We are able to understand the fictive background well enough to see that it does illustrate these two statements, although it seems clear that the poet's intended readership understood the poem as alluding to a story they already knew. As W. W. Lawrence wrote eighty years ago, "It must be conceded that some such story [from a heroic tale such as the Offa saga] is far more likely to form the basis of the lyric than an imaginary train of events concocted in the brain of some modern critic" ("Banished Wife" 405).

However confusing the facts of the speaker's situation may be, the imagery is clear and unified. Death is mentioned twice: the speaker's lover is "morþor hycgendne" [thinking of death, 20b] and they vowed "þæt unc ne gedælde nemne deað ana" [that nothing but death alone could separate them, 22]. The speaker walks before dawn, lives in a pagan shrine, in some kind of underground dwelling that, if it is not a grave, certainly resembles one. The description of the lover's circumstances—sitting passively in a hall surrounded by water and frosted by the storm—suggests, if not states, that he is dead. None of these instances alone proves that either the speaker or her lover is dead, nor do they together. The function of these death images, beyond creating a mood of horror, may be to illustrate the association of paganism with death for the Christian author of this lyric and for his readers.[11] In any case, the pagan imagery must have been just as chilling as the death imagery for the poet's intended audience, and all of it contributes to the emotional response that the poem evokes in the reader. The imagery is so thoroughly claustrophobic that reading the poem almost suggests the sensation of being buried alive. As in "Wulf," the strong emotions that the speaker stirs in us prepare us to accept the truth of the poem's gnomic conclusion: "Wa bið þam þe sceal of langoþe leofes abidan."

"Deor" is one of only two Old English poems spoken by a *scop,* the other being the mnemonic "Widsið." Like "The Wife's Lament," "Wulf," and "Resignation," "Deor" is spoken by a fictive character in a concrete and specific situation which illustrates an aphorism. The poem begins with five brief allusions, in the nonpersonal voice, to narratives that all scholars agree were well known to the poet's contemporaries, followed by a short segment on the thoughts of one afflicted with sorrow, also in the third person, and finally a first-person section in which the speaker gives his name and his situation. Although this scheme would not seem to promise a lyric poem, "Deor" nevertheless is fully lyrical because the cumulative effect of the six narratives (Deor's own and the five others) is the communication of an emotional response to these tales.

The relationship among the poet, the speaker, and the character Deor is a troublesome one, since we cannot even be certain whether *deor* "bold" or "a wild animal" was intended as a proper name. Animal names were common among Scandinavian singers as cognomens (Lawrence, "Song" 19), but the sentence "Me wæs Deor noma" [*deor* was my name, 37b] could be read figuratively as "you could have grouped me with the merely appetitive creatures of the world" (Bolton, "Boethius" 227). It seems best, however, to continue to refer to the speaker as Deor, with the understanding that the preterite tense in this sentence suggests that this was not his given name.

If the speaker's name is in doubt, his relationship to the poet is even more so. Two studies made in the 1960s suggest the difficult notion that the poet, or *scop*, is speaking *in propria persona*, but that the character of Deor is a mask. Norman Eliason reads "Deor" as a *scop*'s begging poem, and believes that the character Deor "is intended . . . to serve as the poet's alter ego" ("Two" 187).[12] Eliason is right to notice the duality of Deor's character—on the one hand "life-like" and on the other "utterly incredible" (187). Morton Bloomfield, in an essay that reads "Deor" as a charm against misfortune, also believes the character to be a persona of the speaker-poet: "It is possible that the singer Deor was well-known as an escaper of misfortune, and the poet assumed his mask to write his sophisticated charm or shifted into his role in only one stanza" (226). This suggestion, that Deor was a legendary *scop,* is a good one, and does not depend on understanding the poem as a charm. Most other scholars have understood Deor as a fictive character,[13] although at least one modern student of the poem hedges on the fictiveness of Deor: Jerome Mandel calls the first-person section "an intimate revelation of his own (or his persona's) affliction, albeit fictionalized," and then adds in a footnote that the question of fictiveness is irrelevant: "The point is that the story is supposed to be accepted by the listeners as true" (2).

It seems to me that whether Deor is the poet's persona or an fictive speaker depends on how the poem's origin and transmission are understood. The exceedingly tight thematic structure of the six narrative sections and the formal suspense that they create for the revelation of the speaker's name indicate a lettered composition made in leisure and reflection, not a transcription of a *scop*'s occasional effort. It seems best, therefore, to grant that Deor, or the person for whom Deor was a cognomen, was a figure of some importance for the Anglo-Saxons, whether he was a historical or legendary character. That Deor was thought to be the author of the poem is unlikely.

The so-called refrain of the poem is usually seen as the key to both theme and structure. The line "Þæs ofereode, þisses swa mæg" [that passed, so can this] occurs six times, once after each of the first five narrative allusions, and again as the last line of the poem. Clearly, this line is not a refrain in the technical sense since the poem, like all Old English poems, is not stanzaic (that is, verse lines are grouped, if grouped at all, by idea rather than by metrics) and the repeated line does not function as a metrical device. It is merely a repeated line, which functions thematically rather than formally.[14] Unfortunately, its meaning is far from clear to us. In the first five appearances, the line seems to mean "That misfortune I have just related to you passed; this misfortune, my own, can, too." However, to read the last occurrence, which follows Deor's own misfortune, in the same way is impossible: if *þisses* refers to Deor's misfortune in the first five instances, it cannot refer to the same thing in the last. Some scholars suppose that *þisses* refers in every instance to whatever misfortune the reader may find herself in, while others accept a change in referent for the last occurrence. The *þæs* also poses a problem in that several of the misfortunes in the five narratives are clearly permanent: thus, we must either understand the thing that passes to be the mental anguish rather than the misfortune itself, or we must assume that the passing of misfortune is actually the death of the unfortunate one. All these quandaries are more than merely lexical uncertainties, for they bear upon the meaning of the repeated line, and of the poem as a whole. That is, if the line is interpreted as optimistic, then the speaker offers consolation, but if the line is understood as a reference to the release of death, then the speaker offers stoic endurance.[15]

The meditative section of the poem is likewise uncertain:

> Mæg þonne geþencan,   þæt geond þas woruld
> witig dryhten   wendeþ geneahhe,
> eorle monegum   are gesceawað
> wislicne blæd,   sumum weana dæl.

(31–34)

[One can then think that the wise Lord wends constantly throughout this world, to many an earl shows honor and certain fame, to others a portion of woes.]

This sentence could mean either that God changes men's fortune, or that he does not. One wonders if it is possible that the Anglo-Saxons could have understood this sentence and the repeated line without some external information that we lack. The solution to the uncertainties of the repeated line and the meditative section most likely lies in the story of Deor. If only we knew what happened to him at this point in his career, we would know whether the poet's theme is the eventual turn of fortune for the better, or the hope of eternal bliss. Thus, the character Deor must have provided the meaning of the philosophical theme of the poem, as well as that of the emotional response to the narratives.

The relationship among the six narrative sections is also best approached from the point of view of Deor. I believe we can safely disregard one scholar's statement that "the final section of the poem as we have it [Deor's own story] was in the nature of an afterthought or postscript" (Malone, *Deor* 15). P. J. Frankis was the first to note the now generally accepted idea that "the first five sections of the poem have a special connexion with the story of Deor" (167).[16] The narrative sections are summarized as follows: 1) Weland [the elf smith of Germanic legend] suffered hardship when Nithhad made him prisoner; 2) Beadohild [Nithhad's daughter] found her pregnancy more grievous than the death of her brothers [for all of which Weland was responsible]; 3) an obscure section which may refer either to the love of Maethhild and Gaut, a harper who charmed his dead wife out of the water in which she drowned, or to Nithhad again, "the Geat" who suffered from the "harvest of battle" (mæð hilde");[17] 4) Theodric [probably, but not certainly, the Visigoth responsible for Boethius's death] ruled a city for thirty years; 5) Eormanric, the tyrant king of the Goths, was cruel to many men; 6) I, Deor, lost my position as *scop* at the court of the Hoedenings to Heorrenda.

Although much of this is obscure to us, it is nevertheless possible to make some plausible connections among at least most of these six stories. For example, James L. Boren postulates that Weland is a creative artist, Beadohild the passive antitype of the artist, Geat the artist and Maethhild the antitype, and Theodric a well-known persecutor of the artist Boethius (270). He believes the point of these stories to lie in the power of the artist to overcome adversity, which is what the artist Deor hopes to do. Edward I. Condren takes a different tack, finding that the first three stories each concern a protagonist who is a creator (Weland and Gaut are artists, while Beadohild is "creating," by gestating, the hero Widia), while the fourth and fifth concern antagonistic kings, and the sixth, Deor's story, "describes a classic confrontation between scop and lord in which the scop triumphs . . . through the artistry of the very poem we are studying" (64). Thomas T. Tuggle concentrates on the Weland story as the topic of the first three sections, pointing out that both Weland and Deor "are artists and have endured insensitive treatment from a king" (237). Although these three interpretations present mutually exclusive ways in which the reader may make connections between Deor's story and the five others, it seems clear that some such connection is implicit in the text. In each of these three readings, the first five narratives would have prepared the intended reader for the sixth.

The reader is surely to make some connection between Deor and Weland. The speaker tells us twice that Weland endured *wræc* "misery" or, more particularly, "exile" which Deor, having been sacked, must also endure. The story of Beadohild, though, points up the difference between Deor and Weland. While the smith Weland raped Beadohild and killed her brothers in revenge for their father's treachery, the poet Deor not only sympathizes with her plight, but also forgoes any vengeance of his own. If we take the third story to concern Nithhad (rather than Gaut) we find sympathy for the persecutor, too. In other words, the speaker first identifies himself with Weland as an artist wronged and capable of vengeance through his art, and then sympathizes with Weland's victims. If, on the other hand, the third story is understood as concerning the harpist Gaut, we find another instance of the speaker's concern with the power of the artist to deal creatively with adversity. The fourth and fifth stories present more general concerns, the hardships of many in the face of a king's tyranny, although the fourth may be a specific reference to the execution of Boethius. These five stories, however imperfectly we understand them, demonstrate a purposeful thematic connection with the speaker's own story. Furthermore, the course of these stories is dynamic: they take the speaker from a close identification with Weland, whose only reaction to his misfortune is vengeance, through empathy for his victim or victims, to a larger understanding of the hardships many people must face.

Deor's character thus provides the connections among, and the poet's choice of, the narrative sections. In all of these, his role as *scop* is paramount. The poem includes bits of Germanic legend, European history, and gnomic wisdom, all the stock in trade of an Anglo-Saxon *scop*. And since his story, the keystone to the poem, is not given until the very end, he has succeeded in his role as *scop* by involving the reader or auditor in the poem and its solution. It would not be far-fetched to think of this poem as riddle-like in that the reader is challenged to guess the speaker's identity before the end of the poem. Of course, "Deor" is not really a riddle, but it invites the audience to participate in much the same way, and one can imagine that many members of this poet's audience would not have been at all surprised to learn that the speaker was the *scop* Deor. Each of these allusive narratives illustrates the repeated aphorism, and the cumulative effect of all six draws the reader into feeling the truth of it himself.

To summarize the effect of using an individual fictive speaker, we can say that although the fragmentary condition of "Resignation" makes it impossible for us to guess what the poet expected his readers to know of the speaker's story, if anything, it seems clear that authors of "Wulf," "The Wife's Lament," and "Deor" depend heavily upon the reader's prior familiarity with their fictive speakers. These three poems probably, and "Resignation" possibly, make use of received narratives in order to illustrate an aphorism or aphorisms. The type characters of "The Seafarer" and "The Riming Poem," however, are not likely to have been adopted from a received narrative, although they may certainly have been current in folk wisdom, for each is too general and vaguely sketched to have indicated much else to the poem's intended readership than the likelihood that the speaker was to be understood figuratively.

One critic has described the little read and very difficult "Riming Poem" as "a lunatic exercise" (Pearsall 73)—a typical response to the frustration the modern reader feels over the poem's metrical scheme, which is bound by both strict alliteration (*both* stressed syllables of the on-verse alliterate with the first of the off-verse) and by the riming of the last word of the on-verse with that of the off-verse, which rime is frequently carried over into the next line. This double constraint of alliteration and rime has necessitated some unusual constructions and diction, thus obscuring the sense for us non-native readers of Old English. The following discussion relies heavily on O. D. Macrea-Gibson's text: all quotations and the verse translations are from his edition.

In the wonderfully condensed opening line, the speaker presents himself and a major theme of the poem: "Me lifes onlah se þis leoht onwrah" [To me he offered life who showed forth the light]. Thus, the speaker presents himself as merely one of God's vast creation, but he expresses this idea in such a way that it implies some sort of special status. This odd paradox is continued in the next few lines:

glæd wæs ic gliwum,   glenged hiwum
blissa bleoum,   blostma heowum.

(3–4)

[I was glad, rejoicing, arrayed in the hues
of delight, of the flowers of the field.]

Here, although his joy is like the colors of field flowers, and thus at one with nature, the image hardly makes him typical of mankind. This very special and privileged person, for whom nature was fruitful and men happy (lines 5–12), finally reveals his station in life in lines 15ff: he was a king praised and protected by his retainers, and at one with nature: "swylce eorþe ol; ahte ic ealdorstol" [Even thus the earth gave harvest, and I held the high seat (i.e., "throne"), 23]. The theme of the connection between human society and nature is continued: the harp resounded in both hall and sky (lines 27–30), and the king protected both earth and people (40). But this happy and harmonious state in which man and nature are one, the subject of the first 42 lines, is described completely in the past tense. One spot in this section hints at the reason that the speaker's present situation is far different: all this was true "þenden wæs ic *in* mægen" [while I was in my strength, 18b].

Then at line 43, which begins with the word *nu* "now," the verb tense changes to the present, the first person pronouns are replaced by the third person, and the topic changes from harmony and joy to fear, evil, death, pain, and ruin. Nature continues in sympathy with the speaker: "sumurhat colað, foldwela fealleð" [the heat of summer cools, the land's good fails, 67b–68a]. The two stages of the speaker's life are likened to day and night: "Gewiteð nihtes in fleah se ær in dæge wæs dyre" [What was precious in the day flees away in the night, 44b–45a]. There is no indication whatever of what has caused this turn of events: all we are told is that "Flah is geblowen" [Evil has bloomed, 47b]. When the speaker reverts to first person constructions in line 70, it is to make the chilling observation that "Me þæt wyrd gewæf ond gewyrht forgeaf þæt ic grofe græf," [for me fate wove this, gave this to do, to carve out a grave, 71–72a]. This image of the speaker digging his own grave concludes his description of the night of his life, and leads him to his final remarks, beginning in line 79b, that man is more truly protected and happy in heaven. In the very last sentence (83bff) we find ourselves included in the speaker's thoughts by his *uton* construction: "then let us hasten" to heaven.

"The Riming Poem" is surely general in topic, if not plainly vague, and its speaker a type character. So general is the situation that one critic wonders if the speaker is a man at all, and ventures the guess that he represents something like the will of God (Lehmann "Old English" 440). Clearly he is not meant to be a specific person: the fact that he is a king is not an attempt to specify or individuate, but rather is a function of the sympathetic relationship he has with nature. Since the king's decline is mirrored by the decline both of the year and of human prosperity, one could say either that the speaker personifies his realm, or conversely, that his realm responds to his health, something in the manner of the Waste Land of the Fisher King. He is so closely associated with both the natural world and the world of human society that he takes on nearly mythic proportions. The *uton* construction of the last sentence should therefore come as no surprise: one who personifies or precipitates the decline of both the natural and the human spheres of life on earth surely has the authority to exhort us to eternal salvation. Far from indicating a new voice, the use of the inclusive first-person plural is the natural culmination—and purpose—of the association among the speaker, the natural world, and human society that the poem has so carefully built up.

The nearly complete absence of any narrative background and the absence of any specifics of the speaker's character are balanced, however, by great specificity in imagery. For example, the speaker appears to the reader's inner eye arrayed in the hues of flowers (quoted above, 3–4), his kinship bonds give him nourishment (24b), a burning treasure blooms in his breast (46), his death day comes swift as an arrow (72b), and so on—the examples are too numerous to rehearse. This deftly handled imagery enables the poet effectively to convey the speaker's emotional response to his decline, in spite of the vagueness of his character and background. The wonder of the poem is that despite the difficult prosody and the absence of any concrete details concerning the speaker and his situation, it should be so beautiful and haunting. "The Riming Poem" thus dramatically exemplifies how a lyric poem can virtually glamour the reader by breaking through ontological boundaries: the reader identifies with the speaker in his old age who is identified with the physical world in the Last Days. The modern reader need not be a Christian—or an Anglo-Saxon—to assent to the observation of the darkness and decline of our world relative to some imagined Golden Age in the past, the youth of our culture. The Christian exhortation with which this poem ends provides one response—the Anglo-Saxon response—to a desperate situation.

The poet of "The Seafarer" set himself a less difficult task, choosing conventional prosody and a speaker with whose more realistic situation the intended reader must have had some ready sympathy. Nevertheless, it has a great deal in common with "The Riming Poem": great specificity of nature imagery, an important role for the pathetic fallacy, a sketchy background for the speaker, a lengthy lapse into the third-person, a first-person plural close that constitutes the only recognition of the poet's audience or readership, and a nearly identical topic—the transience of earthly life.

"The Seafarer" comes to us today trailing a great train of modern scholarship and criticism behind it, much of it having to do with the speaker or speakers of the poem. Unfortunately for the present purpose, however, this body of writing has sought chiefly to establish the number of speakers and the delineations of their utterances, and rarely ventures on the nature of the speaker, or on any further implications he may have for the poem.[18] Scholarly consensus (and common sense) having settled on a single speaker, the modern reader's task is to follow that speaker through several abrupt shifts of tone which take the poem from a vivid and concrete description of seafaring to an exhortation that we all turn our thoughts to heaven.

The speaker begins with a claim to be relating an actual experience, much like the speaker of "The Wife's Lament": "Mæg ic be me sylfum soðgied wrecan" [I can tell a true story about myself, 1]. Moreover, the vivid language and imagery in the first 33 lines contribute to the sense of a real experience. The setting is specific: the speaker's hardships take place during night watch, in the winter, by cliffs, in the ship's prow (through line 8). And his hardships are specific: he is cold, grieving, hungry, and lonely (through line 26). But these specific details are presented for the most part figuratively, for nearly everything the speaker mentions is personified. Frost bound his feet with cold fetters, cares sighed, hunger bit him—even the world *cearseld* (5b) denotes the 'abodes of sorrows,' which the speaker figuratively visits. The memorable lines about the sea birds (19b–26) provide a good example of the way in which the speaker joins specific and realistic detail with powerful figurative language:

>   Hwilum ylfete song
> dyde ic me to gomene,   ganetes hleoþor
> ond huilpan sweg   fore hleator wera,
> mæw singende   fore medodrince.
> Stormas þær stanclifu beotan,   þær him stearn oncwæð

isigfeþera;   ful oft þæt earn bigeal,
urigfeþra;   ne ænig hleomæga
feasceaftig ferð   frefran meahte.

(19b–26)

[At times I made the song of the whooper swan entertainment for myself, the cry of the gannet and the voice of the curlew I made the laughter of men, the singing seagull I made the mead drinking. There storms beat against the stone cliffs, there the icy feathered gull replied. Often the dewy feathered eagle screamed round about: no protecting kinsman could console my desolate spirit.]

Margaret Goldsmith, in her study of "The Seafarer and the Birds," has identified each of the species (I have used her identifications in the translation above), showing that all of them are commonly found along the coastal areas of England during the winter and that the characteristic cry of each is appropriate to the associations the speaker makes in these lines. However, along with the explicit realism of this section is the moving image of the birds as the speaker's companions and kinsmen.

These extremely vivid lines draw the reader into an empathetic identification with the seafarer and his physical sufferings on the sea. Although much of this seems to the modern reader to be grossly exaggerated, the concreteness and detail nevertheless clearly communicate his suffering. Having empathized thus far, however, we are greatly surprised at line 33:

Forþon cynssað nu
heortan geþohtas,   þæt ic hean streamas,
sealtyþa gelac   sylf cunnige;

(33b–35)

[And yet my heart's thoughts urge that I try the high seas, the tossing of the salt waves, for myself.]

From here through line 64, the speaker expresses his apparently unmotivated compulsion to set to sea, leaving the pleasures of a spring landscape and human society (including thoughts "to wife wyn" [of the joy of a woman, 45a]) behind him.

Despite the wealth of detail, the speaker remains a vague figure, much like the king of "The Riming Poem." And like the king, the seafarer is strongly connected with nature, particularly as it reflects his mood. When he is oppressed with cares, "hægl scurum fleag" [hail flew in showers, 17b], but when he looks forward to his sea journey, orchards set blossoms and fields grow beautiful (48–49). Alvin A. Lee interprets this springtime image thus: "The images of a resurgent nature—groves breaking into blossom, the strongholds becoming fair, the plain quickening with springtime vegetation (48–49)—are the conventional symbols associated with Old English paradisal and redemptive themes and are intimations of the desired state which is not yet his" (145). Other images in this passage (33b–64a) support a symbolic reading. For example, although the language grows gradually more general, there is the striking image of the cuckoo:

> Swylce geac monað   geomran reorde,
> singeð sumeres weard,   sorge beodeð
>
> (53–54)

[The cuckoo, the keeper of summer, sings, exhorts with sad voice, bodes sorrow.]

Here, the realistic detail of the sad sound of the cuckoo's call in summer is combined with the figurative function of the cuckoo as the announcer of death (O. S. Anderson 26). The lines on the soul's flight are a second example:

> Forþon nu min hyge hwerofeð   ofer hreþerlocan,
> min modsefa   mid mereflode
> ofer hwæles eþel   hweorfeð wide,
> eorþan sceatas,   cymeð eft to me
> gifre ond grædig,   gielleð anfloga,
>
> (58–62)

[But yet now my thought turns throughout my breast, my mind turns with the sea flood, widely over the whale's homeland to every corner of the earth. Afterwards, it comes back to me ravenous and greedy; the lone flier yells.]

The power of the lines concerning the speaker's soul ranging out over the sea depends upon the soul's presentation as a bird, much like the birds in 19b–26, while yet perhaps intended to be taken literally as an instance of the "belief in the soul's ability to leave the body during life and to return again" (Salmon 2 and Henry *Early*

137–51). The nature imagery in this passage would have had conventional allegorical connotations for the poet's intended readers, leading them to expect the crux at line 64 in which the topic appears, to us, to change from seafaring to man's life on earth.[19] "The Seafarer" thus exhibits the homiletic structure that we have observed throughout this discussion of fictive speakers. This poem, however, employs conventional Christian symbols to illustrate its Christian aphorism.

Continuing from the lines on the soul quoted above, the transition from vehicle to tenor, from concrete to abstract, from *exemplum* to explanation, is made thus:

> gielleð anfloga,
> hweteð on hwælweg   hreþer unwearnum,
> ofer holma gelagu.   Forþon me hatran sind
> dryhtnes dreamas   þonne þis deade lif,
> læne on londe.   Ic gelyfe no
> þæt him eorðwelan   ece stondað

(62b–67)

[the lone flyer (i.e., his thought or soul) yells, irresistibly incites my heart to the whale-way, over the expanse of the sea. Thus, the Lord's joys are hotter to me than this dead, transitory life on earth. I do not believe that the earth's wealth stands eternal.]

If we understand the seafaring figuratively as the journey of life, this crux makes a natural and logical transition. The final lines, beginning "Uton we hycgan hwær we ham agen" [Let us now think about where we may possess a home, 116] are in what Rosemary Woolf calls "pure sermon style" (205), and it is here, as in "The Riming Poem," that we finally learn whom the speaker is addressing: us.

Looking back over the poem then, we read it as the utterance of one speaker, who appears first as a typical but vaguely sketched seafarer,[20] perhaps too typical to function only as such, but who in the course of the poem takes on the larger proportions of the representative of man in the physical world until he has subsumed even us, the readers. Beginning in isolation, he ends surrounded by the human community, whom he addresses in the final lines. In the first half of the poem, he tells us his situation and his emotions—that he was miserable sailing about the cliffs (1–33a) until he decided to make the journey out of the high seas (33b–64a); in the second half, he tells us what that story means—that we are all in exile here on earth, in an alien and hostile environment, and that we can change our attitudes from complaint to joyous expectation if only we look forward to another life beyond the grave. By making use of a figurative speaker who is also convincing and engaging, as the seafarer is, the poet can enlist his readers' sympathy for such a character to make his point all the more clearly, effectively, and immediately.

The individual speakers of "Resignation," "Wulf," "The Wife's Lament, and "Deor" exemplify the fictive speaker who is a particular person, probably well known to the poems' intended readers. Our inability to understand fully the situations of each of these speakers is surely to be attributed to our lack of prior knowledge of the stories of each, for each provides a wealth of detail on his or her background and personal outlook. There is no sense that the speaker or poet is being deliberately vague, nor is there any sense that any of the details carry allegorical freight, or that they are symbols pointing to some larger meaning. The two women speakers, it is true, are in very close touch with nature—the pathetic fallacy plays a major role in both "Wulf" and "Wife's Lament"—but this nature imagery seems only to dramatize their sorrowful plights rather than to pull them into a larger context as symbols of abstract concepts. This is perhaps only a subjective statement, but it seems plain that when rainy weather accompanies the weeping of Wulf's lover, or when the wife's sexual longing is parallel with her situation in a solitary valley, these images merely dramatize grief and longing, while the perpetual winter in which the seafarer lives does more than dramatize his state of mind—it encourages him to turn his thoughts to eternal bliss.

Each of the four individual characters ends his or her poem with a gnomic statement that is so pat it seems not so much to sum up the situation as to have called up the character and implied the story that precedes it. The statement that, for one who cannot change what is to be, it is best to suffer well ("Resignation" 117–18) sounds much like a bit of folk wisdom that has been neatly illustrated by the story of a self-centered, self-pitying character who refuses even to try. The statement that man can easily put asunder an unsanctified marriage ("Wulf" 18–19) is doubtless an inversion of the biblical statement, and appears here well illustrated by the story of Wulf's unfortunate lover. The two gnomic statements in "The Wife's Lament"—that one must put a good countenance on sorrow, and that one who must endure longing for a loved one has a life of woe—seem also to be folk wisdom (in fact, the first is virtually identical to the aphorism of "Resignation"), and both are again appropriately illustrated by the tale of the unnamed lord and lady of the poem. The repeated aphorism in "Deor," "That passed, this will, too," seems to arise from Deor's own situation and to have called up the other five narratives that illustrate its truth. In each of these four poems, the poet's task is to present the speaker with enough detail to ensure that the reader will recognize her or him, perhaps reminding readers of the outline of the story while at the same time engaging the reader in the speaker's emotions. The poet has then briefly to state the point of the story, the reason for presenting this material. Merely reminding the reader about the story of Wulf and his lover in order to illustrate the closing statement does not make a successful poem: demonstrating the woman's grief over her plight does.

The four lyrics using individual speakers have in their backgrounds closed fictions. The reader of these poems has merely to accept the concept of the character speaking from his or her situation in folktale or literature, and need not make any further adjustment than to accept that the speaker is sufficiently aware of the significance of his or her story to present the moral at the end. These poems transcend boundaries of time ("Deor") or of the human and nonhuman worlds, encouraging the reader who is in another time, place, and situation to empathize with the speakers, but they do not transcend the boundaries between the physical and the spiritual. We can identify with each of these speakers because we have all experienced injustice, loneliness, or sexual longing at one time or another, not because they present any larger view of the human experience. "The Riming Poem" and "The Seafarer," on the other hand, are metaphoric. The absolutely parallel and pointedly described relationships that the king enjoys with both the natural world and with human society are not simply a collection of parallels that dramatize his present plight, but are rather the poem's pervasive metaphors, functioning to lift the king out of any individuality the reader might perceive and into the realm of the symbolic. That this is so is supported both by the lack of any background narrative whatever and by the absolutely unrealistic nature of the details of his situation. We therefore can identify with the king and his anguish not because we have experienced a similar situation but because he presents metaphorically the *human* situation. The seafarer enjoys much the same kind of relationship with the natural world—the parallels between his life and the physical world are pervasive and apparently enduring, just as the king's are. His sketchy background also supports the conception that he is a figure, or metaphor. But, unlike the king, the seafarer has something of the realism found in the individual speakers. The king functions only as the personification of his earthly realm—he has no other reality—but the seafarer functions not only as the representative of man in the physical world, but also as a seafarer—in fact, he begins by convincing the reader that this is so, and that he has a true story to tell about his sufferings. We identify with the seafarer, as we do with the king, not because we have been in his situation, but because he symbolizes the human situation.

The fictive speakers are thus successful both in conveying the emotional responses of their speakers to their subjects, and in illustrating their gnomic conclusions, and this is true whether the speaker is a particular individual, like Deor, the two women, and the unpleasant fellow of "Resignation," or an obvious metaphor, like the king, or a figurative character who partakes of the concrete, like the seafarer. In "The Wanderer" and "The Dream of the Rood," which are discussed in the last chapter, the poets have taken one large step beyond the possibilities offered by the fictive speaker, producing poems that rival the depth and sophistication of the English lyric of any period.

6
The Personal Speaker

Chapter 1 discussed at length the reasons we should not expect to find many instances of the personal speaker in early medieval poetry. Early manuscript cultures like that of Anglo-Saxon England retain many features of oral cultures. Their poetry is traditional and, like modern folk art, is understood to generate from the memory and experiences of the *ethnos* rather than from that of the individual. Furthermore, early manuscript cultures have not yet fully developed the modern concept of self, which requires the objectivity and distance that literacy gradually introduces in a manuscript culture. Since so little of the vernacular poetry of the Anglo-Saxons has survived down to our era, it is impossible to say just how much or how little of it was generated as personal utterances of the poets, but of the extant corpus, only one manuscript epilogue and the four lyric epilogues of Cynewulf's poems have any markings of being personal, individual communications from the poet to his readers.

The epilogue to ms. 41 and Cynewulf's epilogues have three things in common. First, they are without doubt intended to be read rather than heard. The manuscript epilogue has no raison d'etre exclusive of its position in its manuscript, and Cynewulf's epilogues contain runic characters which function not only as graphemes to spell his name, but also as words in the text of the poems. It would be impossible for any listener who has not seen the manuscript to be able to discover the signature. Second, the manuscript epilogue and Cynewulf's lyric epilogues to "Fates of the Apostles" and *Juliana* expressly ask their readers to pray for the poet who wrote them. Perhaps it was this Christian concept of individual salvation that suggested the novel idea of the poet speaking in his own person and, in the case of Cynewulf, of signing his own name. The poems, then, like the salvation they aim to effect, originate in the individual consciousness rather than in the ethnic consciousness. Once this concept is introduced, it is a short and logical step to the modern concept of written discourse as the property of the author and of its function as the extension of the author's own character and purposes. In any case, these poems were written in explicit expectation of a readership comprised of persons unknown to the poet—a truly modern concept. Third, each of these poems is attached in some way to an objective reality outside the communication between speaker and addressee in the lyric. The epilogue to ms. 41 depends upon the existence of the manuscript, and Cynewulf's lyric epilogues are attached to poems that are more or less narratives, which, as we have seen in chapter 1, establish objective realities to which the events of the narratives refer. Furthermore, Cynewulf's poems refer to objective worlds that were supposed to be factual and historical. The narratives concern unique events—the lives of Juliana and Elene, the Ascension, and the acts of the apostles—which have grave significance for Christians. Both the works of verbal art written in ms. 41 and the events of Cynewulf's narratives have been hypostatized, made into objects that are manipulable by the scribe or poet. It is not surprising, then, that it occurs to these two writers to address their readership in the personal voice, since the concept of authorship develops with the hypostatization of the poem.

The manuscript epilogue mentioned above appears in ms. 41, Corpus Christi College, which comprises a copy of the Alfredian translation of Bede's *Ecclesiastical History* and many marginal texts, including a portion of *Solomon and Saturn*. This lyric epilogue is spoken by an *ic* who identifies himself immodestly as "þone writre wynsum cræfte þe ðas boc awrat bam handum twam" [the writer of delightful talent who wrote this book with both hands, two of them, 4–5]. Given the contents of the manuscript, this *writere* must be a scribe of either this manuscript or of its exemplar (rather than the author of the entire contents of the books), and it is as much, rather than as the poet, that he speaks to the reader. As the scribe, then, he prays each nobleman who reads the book to promote him (4a) and protect him (6ff) so that he may live righteously and praise God to the end of his days (9–10), a theme that reminds one of that of the prayers discussed in chapter 3, although it is here human rather than divine aid that the speaker seeks this end. It is difficult to understand how this speaker could have expected patronage unless he gave his name somewhere in the manuscript, or unless he were well known to the recipients of the book as the two-handed (ambidextrous?) writer, which latter seems unlikely since he addresses his readers in the most general terms as though he is not certain who they will be. Although this epilogue is of little aesthetic merit, it does illustrate the existence elsewhere of some features usually thought to be unique to Cynewulf's signed corpus.

In referring to Cynewulf's lyric epilogues, I use the term "epilogue" to designate the final segment of each of Cynewulf's signed poems, in distinction to the "signature," which is only a small part of each of the epilogues—the part of the epilogue containing the author's name in runes. *Juliana* and *Elene,* both narrative poems, contain clearly separable lyric epilogues that begin when the narrative ends (in *Elene* the word *finit* occurs immediately before the epilogue), and "The Fates of the Apostles," a short collection of proto-narratives, concludes with an equally clearly separable lyric epilogue. *Christ II,* however, is in the homiletic vein: it is throughout exhortatory and didactic, as well as narrative, and it contains several lyric segments in the form of speeches or songs. The final segment in this poem, then, is not so clearly separable in tone and intent as are the epilogues of the three narrative poems. Nevertheless, it seems best to continue to use the word "epilogue" for the last segment of each poem.

Several features distinguish the epilogues from the poems proper. First, none of the epilogues has a counterpart in the Latin source of each poem (Calder, *Cynewulf* 100). Second, the beginning of each epilogue is clearly marked by a shift from the third person to the first: the word *ic* appears in the first sentence of each. And third, each epilogue contains the only runes in each of the poems.[1] Furthermore, the epilogues share important features: each takes an eschatological theme and follows a pattern in which the first-person voice is succeeded in the signature section by the third-person voice, which in turn is followed by what Kenneth Sisam calls "the quiet close [of] a prayer or its equivalent" ("Cynewulf" 323). The sudden shift to the third person for the section in which Cynewulf reveals his name is somewhat jolting for the reader, although Ralph W. V. Elliott has defended it as "making the runic passages stand out all the more poignantly, thus stressing further their deeper significance" ("Cynewulf's Runes in *Jul* and *Fates*" 204). It is true that the shift in person has this effect, but it seems to be more than an attention-getting device. That Cynewulf will employ the personal voice until he gives his name indicates some uncertainty about asserting himself *in propria persona,* which is understandable given that he is the only poet in the extant corpus of Old English verse whose speaker not only declares that he is the author but also names himself. Of course, Cynewulf was not the only vernacular writer of the early Middle Ages to include his name in his poetry.

The Old High German poet Otfrid signed himself in much the same manner in the epilogue to his *Krist,* giving his name, like Cynewulf, for the stated purpose of gaining the prayers of his readers. This intention is also explicitly stated in the opening lines of the narratives of Hartmann von Aue three centuries after Otfrid. However, neither of these German poets engages in either the rapport with his audience or the self-examination that are characteristic of Cynewulf, and that sometimes lead the reader, anachronistically, to assume that the epilogues are autobiographical.[2]

"The Fates of the Apostles" is the only one of the four signed poems to introduce the poet's voice before the epilogue. In fact, the opening lines proclaim the speaker's authorship and describe his method of composition:

> Hwæt! Ic þysne sang   siðgeomor fand
> on seocum sefan,   samnode wide

[Travel-weary and sick at heart, I composed this song, gathered it from far and wide.]

However, the poem thereafter continues in the non-personal voice, with several insertions of the "we gehyrdon" [we heard] formula, until the opening of the epilogue and the reappearance of the personal speaker:

> Nu ic þonne bidde   beorn se ðe lufige
> þysses giddes begang   þæt he geomrum me
> þone halgan heap   helpe bidde.

(88–90)

[Now I pray the man who loves the study of this song that he pray to the holy band (i.e., the apostles) for help for me in sadness.]

The signature section following is introduced as a riddle:

> Her mæg findan   foreþances gleaw,
> se ðe hine lysteð   leoðgiddunga
> hwa ðas fitte fegde.

(96–98a)

[Here the clever in deliberation who pleases himself with poems may find who composed this fitt.]

and it concludes in the same vein:

> Nu ðu cunnon miht
> hwa on þam wordum wæs   werum oncyðig.

(105b–6)

[Now you may know who was made known to men in these words.]

Then, in what looks like an alternate version of the beginning of the epilogue, the speaker again asks the reader for aid at his death. The poem ends with an exhortation in the first-person plural.

In "Fates," for all that it uses the personal speaker, the emphasis is on the audience, and on the poet's relationship to them. The riddle-like frame of the signature section is, in Dolores Warwick Frese's words, an "invitation to the reader to participate in the compositional act," and the introduction of the "we" in line 115 "subtly incorporates each nameless reader into the poem" ("Art" 320).[3] However, not every chance reader is included in Cynewulf's address. Three times he limits his intended audience to "foreþances gleaw" [the clever in deliberation, 96b] and "beorn se ðe lufige þysses giddes begang" [the man who loves the study of this song, 88b–89a], which is repeated nearly verbatim in verses 107b–8a. Cynewulf addresses only the intelligent and scholarly—that is, men like himself—expecting only these elite readers to pray for him. Nevertheless, the speaker clearly takes great pains to include this limited audience in the poem, and to identify himself with them, making the personal speaker a device for expressing communion between poet and reader.

The speaker of the epilogue to *Juliana* likewise attempts to group himself with his readers, although this is less marked here than in "Fates." The *Juliana* epilogue begins in mid-line, 695b, with a first-person declaration that the speaker will need the help of this saint at his Judgement. This theme is interrupted by the brief third-person signature section, but thereafter continues through 718a, after which the speaker addresses his audience:

> Bidde ic monna gehwone
> gumena cynnes,   þe þis gied wræce,
> þæt he mec neodful   bi noman minum
> gemyne modig,   ond meotud bidde
> þæt me heofona helm   helpe gefremme

(718b–22)

[I pray every person of human race who may recite this poem that he earnestly remain mindful of me by means of my name and pray to God that the Helm of the Heavens give me help.]

He then concludes with a prayer for God's mercy spoken in the first-person plural.

This speaker does not explicitly identify himself as the author of the poem, although this is clearly implied, but he does identify himself, as in "Fates," as one of the many who need God's mercy (the group idenified as "we"), and, as in "Fates," he has no special relationship to the subject of his poem. Again, what is significant in the speaking voice of this epilogue is his intimate relationship to his audience, rather than to his material. In *Juliana,* his audience is not limited to the clever, but includes everyone who "recites" (i.e., reads aloud) this poem. As in "Fates," the signature is necessary so that the audience can remember him "bi noman minum" [by means of my name, 720b].

The speaker of the epilogue to *Christ II* is somewhat more self-conscious in his role as poet, and sets himself apart from his readers as a special case. The epilogue begins in midline, 789b, with the first-person declaration that the speaker has particular reason to fear Doomsday, since he did not hold properly to biblical teachings. The signature section continues the eschatological theme in the third-person, but the personal speaker reappears in line 815 to explain to the reader why he wrote this poem:

> Forþon ic leofra gehwone   læran wille
> þæt he ne agæle   gæstes þearfe,
> ne on gylp geote,   þenden god wille
> þæt he her in worulde   wunian mote

(815–18)

[Therefore I wish to teach each of those dear to me that he not neglect the needs of the spirit, nor gush with pride when God wills that he dwell here in the world.]

There follows more Doomsday material in the third person, much in the manner of the poem proper, but the epilogue concludes with an exhortation in the first person plural.

In the epilogue to *Christ II,* the speaker singles himself out as both sinner and poet—as one who has particular fears on the subject of the Judgement, and yet who, paradoxically, feels called upon to teach others how to avoid the fears he faces. He addresses his audience in the singular (rather than in the plural as he does in

"Fates" and *Juliana*), as individuals in a group of his intimates, perhaps indicating his expectation of a readership rather than an audience and then finally includes himself in this group in the concluding section. The reader senses an uncertainty in this treatment of the poet's voice: it is as though Cynewulf is not secure in his role as teacher, as though he is here experimenting with such a role. His technique presents the speaker as an individual with a personal relationship to the subject of the poem, but in this epilogue he furthermore presents the members of his audience as individuals with a personal interest in the subject. Thus, he on the one hand sets himself apart as poet-teacher, and on the other treats himself as merely a member of a community to whom the subject of the Judgement is important. As in "Fates" and *Juliana,* Cynewulf's audience is here of great importance to his poetic voice.

The epilogue to *Elene* presents a fuller development of the speaker as poet. It begins:

> Þus ic frod ond fus   þurh þæt fæcne hus
> wordcræftum wæf   ond wundrum læs
> þragum þreodude   ond geþanc reodode
> nihtes nearwe.

(1236–39a)

[Thus I, old and departing from this worthless house (i.e., body), wove verbal arts and collected wonders, at times meditated and arranged my thought in the anxiety of night.]

In this first sentence, the newly presented "I" expressly states that he composed the preceding narrative, and further offers us some information on his method of composition. The rime pattern, which continues (with some variation) through 1250, serves as an additional device to call the audience's attention to the shift from narrative poem proper to lyric epilogue. In this rimed segment, the poet surely is "weaving verbal arts." The rimed section continues in the first person to relate Cynewulf's source of inspiration. He tells us that he had been sinful and in ignorance of the cross until

> . . . me lare onlage   þurh leohtne had
> gamelum to geoce,   gife unscynde
> mægencyning amæt   ond on gemynd begeat,
> torht ontynde,   tidum gerymde,
> bancofan onband,   breostlocan onwand,
> leoðucræft onleac.

(1245–50a)

[the King of Might gave me learning by means of light, a glorious gift as a help for my old age, bestowed, infused in my mind, and revealed clearness; at times opened up, unbound my body, unwound my heart, unlocked the art of song.]

He concludes the first-person section by stating that he had learned about the miracle of the cross in books. The beginning of the signature section is then marked by the usual sudden shift to the third person and by the new topic of the passing of worldly things. The lengthy concluding section shifts to a third topic, Doomsday, still in the third person. This is the only one of the four epilogues in which Cynewulf does not return to the first person after his signature.

This epilogue presents much of the information we have on Cynewulf's speaker. He is old (in this poem, at least).[4] He composes by collecting his material, meditating upon it at night, and versifying it. He had been a sinful man until God gave him wisdom, and simultaneously, artistic ability. He learned about the miracle of the cross from books. Whether all this is true of the poet Cynewulf is irrelevant, but the details are relevant to the speaker, for they establish him as one whose relationship to his material is intimate, personal, and peculiar to him alone. Earl R. Anderson points out the unusual position of the speaker in the body of this poem:

> *Elene* differs from *Ascension* [i.e., *Christ II*], *Fates of the Apostles,* and *Juliana,* where we are continually reminded that a narrator controls the development of the story. In *Elene* Cynewulf has deliberately muted his role as narrator; he has all but disappeared from the poem. His self-effacement in the narrative makes all the more effective his sudden prominence in the epilogue. (115)

The speaker of *Elene,* then, is one who is confident in his poetic voice, in his role as a poet, and in his special relationship to his material.

The four epilogues have so much in common thematically that it is astonishing to observe how greatly they differ with respect to the speaker's voice. In each epilogue the speaker takes a different position vis-à-vis his subject and his audience. It is tempting to see a progression here from "Fates," in which the audience is the prime concern, through *Juliana* and *Christ II* to *Elene,* in which the audience virtually disappears and the subject takes prominence for the speaker. I like to think of Cynewulf having begun to write experimentally to entertain his fellow monks—thus the intimate relationship with his audience and the playful device of inserting his name in "Fates"—and to have gradually come to the realization of a vocation that offered him personal fulfillment—thus his absorption with himself as solitary poet worrying his lines in *Elene*. Although Cynewulf is the only Old English poet to speak to his readers in his own name, these four poems demonstrate that the device of the speaker as poet *in propria persona* was capable of conveying a great variety of stances as the speaker looks both outward to his audience and inward to his subject for his poetic voice.

7

Two Masterpieces

Of the thirty-some Old English poems taken up in this study, two, "The Dream of the Rood" and "The Wanderer," employ speakers who quote or embody other characters or personae, a technique developed by adding the probably novel concept of the personal speaker to frame, enclose, and give additional meaning to the utterance of another, more traditional speaker. In the "Dream," a speaker who is probably to be understood as the poet's persona explicitly quotes a second character, the inanimate rood. The compounding technique in "The Wanderer," however, is more sophisticated: here, a personal speaker does not quote characters who have an independent existence, but rather speaks through two characters who exist only as alternate personae of the personal speaker. The first of these alternate personae, the lordless *eorl,* is modeled on the fictive speaker and in fact greatly resembles the seafarer, while the second, the wiseman, is closer to the personal speaker. "The Dream" and "The Wanderer," then, are quite differently structured and conceived poems. What they have in common is the bold and eminently successful innovation in their speakers, and also, what is surely a related point, their status as acknowledged masterpieces of the Old English lyric.

"The Dream of the Rood" is simply structured, falling naturally into four parts: in the first section, lines 1–27, the dreamer describes both the circumstances in which he met with his dream and the appearance of the rood, ending with the transition, "Ongan þa word sprecan wudu selesta" [Then the best of trees began to speak words, 27].; in the second, lines 28–77, the rood describes its origin as a tree, its ordeal as the instrument of Christ's death, and, briefly, its subsequent burial and rediscovery; in the third, lines 78–121, the rood continues its speech, with a marked change of tone and pronouns, to explain its importance for Christians; and in the fourth and final section, lines 122–56, the dreamer returns to explain the effect this dream had on him, shifting to impersonal constructions at line 147 for a broader picture.[1]

The rood is a very traditional sort of speaker, as we shall see below. The astonishment that modern readers express when they first come upon this poem is clearly anachronistic, for the Anglo-Saxons would have taken both the fact that the rood speaks and the content of its speech in lines 28–77 as matters of course. For one thing, the visionary cross was well established in the popular story of Constantine. In the version of Lactantius—which was perhaps the most widely known in England as it is followed in two Anglo-Saxon homilies (W. Stevens 13) and, of course, in Cynewulf's *Elene*—the cross appears to Constantine not in the heavens but in a dream. Speaking crosses were also well known; for example, that in the apocryphal Gospel of Peter (Henry *Early English* 236). Michael J. Swanton cites two examples: "certain crosses, like that over the gate of Heraclius' palace at Byzantium or another formerly at Glastonbury, were popularly accorded the power of speech" (*Dream* 66). More important than these precedents, however, is the tradition of the inanimate speaker, discussed in chapter 2. As I pointed out there, inscriptions in the voice of the inscribed object were probably the first use to which writing was put, and prosopopoeia remains strong in cultures that are newly literate or craft literate. Prosopopoeia seems to have been particularly thriving in Anglo-Saxon England, for, in addition to epigramatic inscriptions, there are extant riddles, manuscript prefaces, and one lyric poem ("The Husband's Message") that use inanimate speakers, and there are two surviving instances of crosses engraved with prosopopoeic verse. The Brussels Cross, a reliquary probably made in eleventh-century Wessex, reads thus:

> Rod is min nama.   Geo ic ricne cyning
> bær byfigynde,   blode bestemed.
> Þas rode het Æþlmær wyrican and Aðelwold hys beroþor
> Criste to lofe for Ælfrices saule hyra beroþor.

[Rood is my name. I previously bore the powerful king, trembling, wet with blood. Athelmar and his brother Athelwold, in praise of Christ, had this cross made for the soul of their brother Alfric.][2]

The second example is, of course, the Ruthwell Cross. This seventeen-foot stone cross at Ruthwell, Dumfriesshire, bears runic inscriptions that correspond to scattered lines in the second section of "The Dream," the section that comprises the rood's first-person rehearsal of its history. There has been a great deal of speculation about the relationship between the Ruthwell Cross inscription and "The Dream." Dating is of no help in this matter, since, although

the seventh- or eighth-century Ruthwell Cross most likely ante-
dates the Vercelli Book by at least two hundred years, the inscription need not be contemporary with the erection of the cross (Page
150), and the date of the composition of the poem is, in any case,
undeterminable. The text of the inscription does not give the impression of a complete poem, but rather of a series of quotations
from some longer work, generally supposed to be "The Dream"
itself.[3] It is, of course, possible that a stonecutter quoted the poem,
which he may have heard read, but what we know of prosopopoeic
inscriptions suggests that any borrowing was more likely to have
occurred in the opposite direction—the author borrowed from the
stonecutter. Because the correspondence of the two texts is imper-
fect and because they were committed to writing in the northern
and southern extremities of Anglo-Saxon England and probably at
the remove of several centuries from one another, the borrowing is
not likely to have been direct. A plausible explanation would be that
the text of the runic inscription was well known, either circulating
orally or carved on other crosses or both, and that the tenth-
century poet of "The Dream" appropriated it for his poem. To posit
this derivation of "The Dream" is certainly not to deny the poem
artistic unity, or to imply some sort of patchwork construction.
Clearly, the poet of "The Dream" was a poet of genius working with
a well conceived plan for his poem, a plan which would surely have
pleased the poet's intended audience just as we are pleased to
recognize quotations from favorite works in the literature of our
own period.

The rood begins its speech abruptly, despite a careful transition
by the dreamer.

> Ongan þa word sprecan wudu selesta:
> "Þæt wæs geara iu, (ic þæt gyta geman),
> þæt ic wæs aheawen holtes on ende,

$$(27–29)$$

[Then the best of trees began to speak words: "It was a long time ago (I
still remember it) that I was hewn down at the end of the forest.]

This sounds more like the opening of a monologue than the opening
of an address to a specially chosen and very receptive dreamer. In
fact, in this entire second section, the section I postulate to be a
quotation, the rood never indicates that it is addressing anyone at
all, nor that it has any purpose in rehearsing its memories. (When it

does finally address the dreamer, it is at the beginning of the third section, line 78, and this second-person address accompanies a new topic and a new tone.) There are three other curious features in the rood's speech in this section. First, this section is dominated by an odd visual quality. The rood sees Christ approach (33b), sees the earth tremble (36b, where one might expect it to feel rather than see), and sees God suffer (51b–52a). Second, the rood is remarkably passive, not only literally, but grammatically as well. It was cut down, guided, seized, wrought, commanded, borne, set up, and fastened—all this within the space of nine verses (29–33a). The examples of passive constructions and oblique cases of the first-person singular pronoun are too numerous to cite in their entirety, but one example is particularly curious: the rood's response to having nails driven through it is its remark that "On me syndon þa dolg gesiene" [wounds were seen on me, 46b]. One wonders, by whom? Third, the rood sees itself as the protagonist—the victim of the crucifixion rather than the means. Having been forcibly abducted from the forest, it is pierced with nails which open large wounds. All depends on the rood's ability to stand fast in the face of the tortures inflicted on it.

Although the rood seems a curious lyric speaker, much of its character can be attributed to the Anglo-Saxon tradition of inanimate speakers. Its indifference to its audience is reminiscent of the speakers of "Thureth" and "Aldhelm"; its concern with its history and its own importance is similar to that found in all the inanimate speakers discussed in chapter 2, most notably "The Husband's Message"; and its passivity is of course a direct consequence of its nature as an inanimate object.[4]

The dreamer, however, is more problematic. The opening lines, "Hwæt! Ic swefna cyst secgan wylle, hwæt me gemætte to midre nihte" [I want to tell the best dream that I met with at midnight], is reminiscent of the opening lines of the fictive speakers of "The Seafarer" and "The Wife's Lament": "Mæg ic be me sylfum soðgied wrecan" [I am able to deliver a true report about myself] and "Ic þis giedd wrece bi me ful geomorre, minre sylfre sið" [I deliver this story about my very sorrowful self, my own experience]. Furthermore, the probability that the rood's speech, or part of it, was known outside this poem suggests that the Anglo-Saxons would not have understood "The Dream" as the communication of a personal experience. On the other hand, there is much about this speaker, particularly in the fourth section, to remind one of the personal speaker of the epilogue to *Elene*—to wit, his intimate relationship to his subject—and there is no compelling reason to rule out the possibility of a personal utterance, as there is for each of the fictive speakers, for the dreamer is clearly, although not explicitly, a cleric, and thus capable of having composed the poem. It is surely safe to say that the Anglo-Saxon readership was capable of distinguishing between the poet, who did not actually have this particular dream, and his dreamer persona, while yet understanding the poem as a personal communication of the poet's actual devotion to the Holy Cross, which doubtless was shared by many readers.

In the poem's opening line, the dreamer states his motivation: it is his wish merely to communicate the substance of his dream. Yet each detail in the first section is explicitly filtered through the dreamer's perceptions rather than treated as an independent fact. For instance, the dreamer says that "Þuhte me þæt ic gesawe" [It seems to me that I saw, 4] rather than "there was," and he continues this technique with "Geseah ic" [I saw, 14b and 21b], "ic . . . ongytan meahte" [I was able to perceive, 18], "ic . . . beheold" [I beheld, 24–25], and "ic gehyrde" [I heard, 26]. This pattern of filtering the dream through the dreamer performs several functions, of which distancing, the usual explanation given by modern critics for this device, is only a minor one. First, it increases the importance of the dreamer for the reader: the reader is required to engage himself with the dreamer if he wishes to learn about the dream. Another function of this pattern is the way it gives the impression of realism. The visual quality of the first section suggests a real dream (Hieatt 263), and thus prevents the reader from too hastily surmising that the dream is only a conventional device to present a vision. This impression that the dream is actual rather than conventional also increases the prominence of the dreamer, in that it calls the reader's attention to the character to whom this particular dream pertains.

A second device by which the dreamer achieves prominence for himself is that of alternating his perceptions of the dream with his reactions to it. For example, his description of the rood covered with gore is interrupted by his response to the sight: "Eall ic wæs mid sorgum gedrefed, forht ic wæs for þære fægran gesyhðe" [I was all troubled with sorrows, I was frightened before that fair sight, 20b–21a]. When the dreamer reappears in the fourth section, he discusses nothing but his own response to the dream. In these lines he says that he prayed to the rood with great zeal, that the hope of his life is now to worship the rood more than all other men, that most of his friends are dead and that he knows the rood will take him to heaven, and he asks that Christ will be his friend.

Along with this shift in focus from the rood to the dreamer is a shift from contrast between the two to identification. Early in the first section, the dreamer states: "Syllic wæs se sigebeam, ond ic synnum fah" [Wondrous was that victory-tree, and I stained with sins, 13]. This line, which appears at first reading to be a non sequitur, is instead the beginning of a carefully worked out contrast between the dreamer and the rood, a contrast that the poet gradually closes. By the time the dreamer reappears in the fourth section, the contrast is gone. In this section, which includes the dreamer's wish that his devotion to the cross be greater than any other man's, the rood appears not in contrast to the dreamer's sinfulness, but rather as his personal redeemer with whom he now has an empathetic relationship. As the dreamer moves closer to the rood, the audience, with whom the dreamer had shown some concern in his opening section, temporarily disappears. Clearly, the affinities of this section of the dreamer's speech with the epilogue to *Elene* are beyond merely common subject matter. With line 147 the dreamer's "I" disappears, replaced by the first-person plural pronoun that now includes the reader, who was necessarily excluded from the dreamer's personal relationship with the rood. This final section of the poem, however, does not mention the object of the dreamer's devotion, the rood, merely stating that Christ died to redeem "us." Thus the poem begins by positing three distinct points of view: the wondrous cross, the sinful dreamer, and the uninitiated audience. The dreamer's perception then moves closer to that of the cross as he increasingly identifies with it, and away from that of the audience, who have not yet shared his experience. Finally, the audience having experienced the dream vicariously through the poem, the dreamer subsumes himself in the communal "we" and speaks not of the cross but directly of Christ. At this point, his, and our, identification with the cross is complete.

The two speakers, the dreamer and the rood, are thus remarkably similar. Both make use of a predominantly visual perception; both are passive in the face of a spectacle; both are oddly indifferent, given their purposes, to their audience; both are dominated by a sense of their own importance, the idea that each is specially selected over all other men or trees; and finally, of course, both demonstrate an intense need to verbalize their experiences. That these two speakers are so much alike might suggest that the dreamer has projected his own characteristics onto the rood, which, after all, appears only as a figure in his dream. But the features that dreamer and rood share are typical not of the personal speaker, but of the inanimate speaker. Rather than projecting, the dreamer seems to be taking on the rood's features, to be imitating the object of his devotion.

Thus, we have a poem with two speakers—the first an effective combination of aspects of the fictive speaker and the personal speaker, and the second a surprisingly typical example of the inanimate speaker—displaying a tight and sophisticated unity. "The Dream" certainly is a masterpiece of auctorial control over its speakers. What, then, can we say the poem is about? Much has been written about the distance that the poem places between the rood and Christ, between the dreamer and Christ, and, ultimately, between the reader and Christ in a poem that is ostensibly about the Passion. However, this distance seems to be chiefly the result of the employment of a inanimate speaker. When, in the third section, the rood does take up the subject of Christ's sacrifice in earnest, it begins to refer to itself in the third person. Little, if anything, in this poem suggests that it is about the Crucifixion except peripherally. "The Dream" seems to be about the Crucifixion in the same sense that "The Ruin" is about a ruin, or that "The Seafarer" is about seafaring, or that *Beowulf* is about monster-slaying. If Christ is a distant and shadowy figure, then the explanation is that the poem is not about Christ, not that some sort of theological constraints prevented the poet from being more explicit, as is often declared.[5] "The Dream of the Rood" seems rather to be about a man's attempt to assimilate something of profound meaning and importance to himself by means of his literary art, to dramatize a personal devotion to the Cross by means of a metaphoric vision in which his persona takes on the attributes of the object of his devotion—that is, the dreamer becomes very much like the rood.[6] The poem has to do with human perception of divine events, rather than with the divine events themselves, and, more specifically, with one man's highly personal and individualistic attempt to shape his own perception of the mystery of the Cross into a palpable whole with himself firmly at its center. The poet, it seems, wishes to become like the cross, a passive instrument of God's will and the earthly object most closely associated with Christ. Since he is a poet, he does so poetically, and his persona becomes so much like the cross that the rood finally disappears and the dreamer takes its place as a central participant in the central mystery of the Christian faith. And when he does so, he brings the reader with him. The reader begins by sharing the dreamer's sense of sinfulness in the face of the wondrous rood, then vicariously experiences the dream, and then again shares the dreamer's response. As the dreamer grows close to the rood, so does the reader, and when the identification is com-

plete for the dreamer, the reader too feels himself close to Christ
and to the prospect of dwelling with Him eternally in heaven.

As I suggested above, "The Dream," for all its sophistication,
presents a simple method of compounding speakers, for not only is
the technique of one speaker quoting a second a simple one, but the
dreamer is also careful to tell the reader that he is doing just that.
The case of "The Wanderer," however, is far different. Readings
that posit two or more speakers must base their conclusions largely
on the shift in person from first to third, and on the three clauses
that assign lines to perhaps three different speakers: "Swa cwæð
eardstapa" [Thus said the wanderer, 6a]; "Se þonne þisne wealsteal
wise geþohte . . . þas word acwið" [He who thought wisely about
this wall site . . . says these words, 88–91]; and "Swa cwæð snottor
on mode" [Thus the wise one said in his mind, 111a].[7]

Bernard F. Huppé *("Wanderer"),* John Collins Pope ("Dramatic
Voices") and W. F. Bolton ("Dimensions") have all argued for three
speakers—a wanderer, a wise man, and the poet or narrator—but
their divisions of lines among these three are not in agreement:
Bolton gives the poet-narrator the most lines, and Pope the least.
Most who have written on the poem, however, favor some variation
on the two-speaker theory, i.e., that the poem is a monologue by
the wanderer which is introduced and/or interrupted by the poet's
persona, but this reading makes it necessary to understand that the
poet's persona quotes a wanderer who quotes a wise man, which is,
as Bolton says, awkward (12).[8] Thomas C. Rumble, in an excellent
short essay on the poem's structure, avoids the problems of assigning lines and placing quotation marks by assuming a single speaker
who imagines the situations of first the wanderer and then the
ruined wall. Finally, two critics have come out in favor of dropping
the question of speakers altogether: E. G. Stanley suggests that
since the speakers are introduced only to express the poet's theme,
it is not important to determine whether a fictive character or the
poet's persona is speaking in any given line (463); and Rosemary
Woolf *("Wanderer")* makes a similar argument for the irrelevance
of the question. I must agree with Rumble, Stanley, and Woolf that
the poem is best understood as spoken by a single person, and that
that person is not the fictive speaker identified as the wanderer, but
someone very like the poet himself. This speaker sees himself first
as figurative wanderer and then as literal wise man, and speaks as
each of these personae, as well as in his personal voice. However,
these three voices coalesce into one: it is not as though the poet's
persona quotes the wanderer and the wise man, but rather that he

is, or was once, both. Gerald Richman's recent research into the three clauses that identify the speakers demonstrates conclusively that these are "continuing" clauses—that is, clauses that refer both backward to what has just been said and forward to what follows—and that they therefore cannot indicate a change of speaker. Furthermore, the tone is seamless throughout. The speaker's purpose is to describe the transience of the physical world, which he does first from the point of view of a figurative wanderer, and then from that of an older and wiser man, each of whom may be identified with the speaker himself.

Thus, despite the often vivid realism of the poem, the notion that the wanderer has any existence apart from the speaker of the poem as a whole can be safely disregarded, and in this the wanderer differs from the king of "The Riming Poem" and the seafarer: both of these speakers are type characters invented by their authors to convey an idea, but their utterances are free from the intrusions of the poet. The voices in "The Wanderer," however, come and go, always expressing the same theme, but never pausing long enough to make themselves substantial—that is, to really create their fictional backgrounds. Like the authors of these two poems, the author of "The Wanderer" has chosen the homiletic structure to convey his theme. As Stanley says, "The poet is writing on the subjects of mutability and misery, and there are two ways open to him: direct moralizing or the use of imagery. He uses both in this poem" (463). The wanderer is one of his images: the representative of postlapsarian man exiled from Paradise (A. Lee 137 and Smithers 148). However, unlike the seafarer and the king, who control and contain their poems, the wanderer is only one of the poet's complex network of images, to which I now turn.

The poem begins with the image of the wanderer seen as if from afar:

> Oft him anhaga   are gebideð,
> metudes miltse,   þeah þe he modcearig
> geond lagulade   longe sceolde
> hreran mid hondum   hrimcealde sæ

(1–4)

[Often the solitary awaits grace, God's mercy, though, troubled at heart, over the water way he must for a long while stir the frost-cold sea with his hands.]

This picture of the wanderer paddling with his hands in the winter ocean provides one of many realistic details in the image of the wanderer. For example, he himself tells us, in the section that is assuredly to be assigned to him, that he has to tell his troubles when he is alone, not only because he is perpetually alone (as most of the fictive speakers imply) but also because it is the custom of an *eorl* to keep his thoughts to himself (8–18). The speaker confirms that he is an *eorl* in the lines immediately following, saying that he has had these troubles ever since his lord died and he set out "ofer waþema gebind" [over the frozen waves, 24b] to find another (19–29a), which enterprise has apparently not met with success. This rather careful presentation of motivation, to which one may compare the sketchy background of the seafarer, is not, however, realistic, and thus undercuts the realistic story it pretends to account for.[9] As Woolfe points out, there seems to be no reason why the wanderer should not find another *comitatus,* and "certainly there is no reason why the Wanderer should live in a world where the weather is perpetual winter" (*"Wanderer"* 201): to this may be added the improbability of traveling on the frozen sea.

At this point in the poem (beginning at 29b), the first-person constructions are replaced by third-person impersonal constructions, but whether the wanderer is speaking of himself, or of wanderers in general, or whether the poet's persona is speaking of this wanderer, the next topic follows naturally the unrealistic realism of the wanderer's motivation. Here we are told that when the wanderer succumbs to sorrow and sleep,

> Þinceð him on mode þæt he his mondryhten
> clyppe ond cysse, ond on cneo lecge
> honda ond heafod, swa he hwilum ær
> in geardagum giefstolas breac.
> Ðonne onwæcneð eft wineleas guma,
> gesihð him biforan fealwe wegas,
> baþian brimfuglas, brædan feþra,
> hreosan hrim ond snaw, hagle gemenged.

(41–48)

[It seems to him in his mind that he embraces and kisses his lord, and lays his hands and head on his knee, as he enjoyed the throne in former days. When the friendless man afterwards awakens, he sees before him the brown waves, the sea birds bathing and spreading their feathers, the frost and snow falling, mingled with hail.]

This scene has every mark of realism, of a dream or hallucination actually experienced, and is inserted to show how even the great sorrow of the wanderer can be increased by a memory of happier days. Yet the entire scene has the air of the fantastic, and is, after all, only a dream. The scene, and the image of the wanderer, ends with a reference to the wanderer's heart as a bird, an image identical to that in "The Seafarer."

Thus the image of the wanderer, developed over the first 57 lines, partakes of both the concrete and specific, on the one hand, and the fantastic and typical on the other. The wanderer's capacity as a symbol for the fallen world is made in this section by the close association he has with his setting: "night, winter, and chaotic waters are the symbols of the Wanderer's unredeemed or spiritually lost condition" (Alvin Lee 137), but at the same time he himself is, as an exile, a symbol for this condition (Calder "Setting" 271). The time of the wanderer's utterance is *uht* (8b), the hours before daybreak. He is *wintercearig,* "as sad as winter," or "sad because it was winter" (24a), his breast is frozen (33a), and his thought is *hreo,* literally "stormy" (16a), a word used in 105a to modify "hail storm," and thus suggesting that his emotions are analogous to the stormy sea (Irving 160), which is precisely the description given in this section of the weather: "hreosan hrim ond snaw, hagle gemenged" [frost and snow storm down mingled with hail, 48]. While the wanderer is identified with nature, his thoughts are personified. He must fasten his heart with fetters (19–21), sorrow is his companion (30), the exile path attends him (32a), and sorrow and sleep bind him (39–40). The obfuscation of the distinctions among the inanimate, the human, and the intangible is carried out from both ends.

Yet for all the poetic devices that invest the wanderer with the proportions of a symbol, there is much in these lines of overt moralizing, explicit didacticism. The lengthy passage on the "noble custom" of keeping one's thoughts to oneself (11b–18) is one example. Another is,

> Wat se þe cunnað,
> hu sliþen bið sorg to geferan,
> þam þe him lyt hafað leofra geholena.

(29b–31)

[He who experiences sorrow knows how cruel it is as a companion to him who has few beloved protectors.]

These two passages are only small doses of the didacticism to come, however, for the second major image, the ruined wall contemplated by the wise man, is less realistically developed, and hence more open to moralizing.

Beginning on line 58 is a bridge sentence, immediately followed by the second image:

> Forþon ic geþencan ne mæg   geond þas woruld
> for hwan modsefa   min ne gesweorce,
> þonne ic eorla lif   eal geondþence,
> hu hi færlice   flet ofgeafon,
> modge maguþegnas.   Swa þes middangeard
> ealra dogra gehwam   dreoseð ond fealleþ,
> forþon ne mæg weorþan wis   wer, ær he age
> wintra dæl in woruldrice.

(58–65a)

[Therefore, I cannot understand why my heart does not grow dark when I think about the life of *eorls* throughout the world, how they suddenly quit the hall, bold kinsmen and thanes. Thus this earth decays and falls every day; therefore, a man cannot become wise until he has passed many winters in the kingdom of the world.]

In this bridge passage, the same speaker who has been examining the plight of the wanderer, or his own plight as wanderer, turns to the broader subject of the decay of the physical world, and suggests that this broader topic is comprehensible only to the man advanced in age, thus introducing both the image of the crumbling wall and another character, the wise man. The wanderer is called *anhaga* "solitary," *eardstapa* "wanderer," *wineleas guma* "friendless man," and so on, but this new character is called *wita* "wiseman," *gleaw hæle* "clever man," *snottor* "wise one," and so on: clearly the poet is keeping these two distinct. However, since the wanderer's utterance is entirely in the past tense and the wiseman's in the present, and since they are both dependent on the poet's persona, who embodies them, the wanderer and the wiseman appear as two sides of one person—the poet's persona.

Whether the wiseman is identified with the wanderer is not so important as long as one recognizes that the imagery pattern and theme is continuous. In this second segment, the bridge and introduction of a new image and character is followed by some ten lines of gnomic statements that define the wise man, and then, seamlessly, the wasteland is reintroduced:

Ongietan sceal gleaw hæle   hu gæstlic bið,
þonne ealre þisse worulde wela   weste stondeð,
swa nu missenlic   geond þisne middangeard
winde biwaune   weallas stondaþ
hrime bihrorene,   hryðge þa ederas.

(73–77)

[The clever man must perceive how ghostly it is when all the wealth of
this world stands waste, as now here and there throughout the land walls
stand beaten by the wind, fallen upon by frost, the dwellings storm
beaten.]

The ruined city is here explicitly a simile: the future destruction of
the earth is said to be comprehensible to the wise man because it
will be *like* the ruined cities one may see throughout the countryside. The following lines develop this simile, the image of the
decaying wall, by replaying the theme with greater and greater
intensity, introducing winter storms and powerful rhetoric, as in the
well known *ubi sunt* passage:

Hwær cwom mearg? Heær cwom mago?   Hwær cwom maþþumgyfa?
Hwær cwom symbla gesetu?   Hwær sindon seledreamas?
Eala beorht bune!   Eala byrnwiga!
Eala þeodnes þrym!

(92–95a)

[Where went the horse? Where went the young man? Where went the
dispenser of treasure? Where went the seat at feasts? Where are the joys
of the hall? Alas the bright cup! Alas the byrnied warrior! Alas the
prince's might!]

The image of the wanderer was presented in a quasi-realistic manner, but the image of the ruined wall is not given any more reality
than that of the vehicle of a simile. Realism is absent in this section:
the metaphor is all. Yet despite the highly stylized language and
theme, many of the same images encountered in the wanderer
section are present. There is the nature imagery: frost reappears in
verse 78a, and again in the full treatment of the storm in lines 101–
5, replete with the stone cliff and the hail that we remember from
the first section. Furthermore, it is still night: time "genap under
nihthelm" [grew dark under the helm of night, 96a], and even the
nihtscua "night shadow" grew dark (104). This nighttime of the
destruction of the earth corresponds to the nighttime of the wan-

derer's utterance and to our life on earth, which is here called "dark" (89a). A great deal of this imagery is personified. For example, the word *worian* "to move, or totter," is elsewhere used of people but here (78a) of a winehall (Irving 162). Further along, the metaphoric wall "[s]tondeð nu on laste leofre duguþe" [stands now on the tracks of the dear host of warriors, 97], who are now dead. The following lines personify both war and death, and make war and an eorl both grammatically parallel with the two animals:

> Sume wig fornom,
> ferede in forðwege, sumne fugel oþbær
> ofer heanne holm, sumne se hara wulf
> deaðe gedælde, sumne dreorighleor
> in eorðscræfe eorl gehydde.

(80b–84)

[Some war took off, carried away; one a bird bore away from the high sea; one the grey wolf divided with death, one a sad faced *eorl* hid in a grave.]

A final example of the blurring of distinctions among men, beasts, inanimate objects, and abstractions is the identification of man and the wall that the poet makes by placing them twice in the parallel constructions: "Woriað þa winsalo, walend licgað" [The wine-halls fall to ruin, the rulers lie dead, 78] and "Se þonne þisne wealsteal wise geþohte ond þis deorce life deope geondþenceð" [He who wisely thought about this wall-site and deeply thinks through this dark life, 88–89].

The poem comes to a quiet close in the last five lines, which are hypermetric, with the thought that man's real fastness is in heaven. And by the time we reach these lines, we feel that the poet has proven the truth of this statement with his representative wanderer, who guided us through the miseries of a life of exile, and his ruined wall, which served well as a simile for the transience of this world. Despite the many gnomic lines, this poet has succeeded in appealing to the modern taste for showing, not telling, for there is little need for overt moralizing after images such as these. Several critics of the poem have pointed out how the human mind remains in the forefront throughout the poem,[10] and now we have seen why this is so. Rather than speak to us in his personal voice, or in a nonpersonal voice, or in the voice of a fictive speaker, the poet has encompassed all of these in the 115 lines of the poem, forcing us actively to follow his mind as it wanders among the various voices it

has chosen to use. "The Wanderer" makes use of two alternate
personae: the first, the lordless *eorl,* who is, much like the seafarer,
a representative of postlapsarian man and a symbol of the fallen
world, but with not quite as realistic a characterization, and the
second, the wise man, who is completely and pervasively metaphoric, and who, even more than the king of "The Riming Poem,"
seems to live outside of time and physical place to ruminate on his
simile of the crumbling wall. The voices of these two speakers flow
in and out of the poem without clearly delineated beginnings or
endings, and as they do so, they merge with the personal voice of
the poet, who introduces them, comments on them, and ultimately,
becomes them.

Afterword

Harold Godwinsson's encounter with an arrow on 14 October 1066 put a rather abrupt end to the production of vernacular verse by the Anglo-Saxons—or, at least, to the recording of it. By the time vernacular literature re-emerged in England, lyric poetry had become decidedly less alien to modern readers than the lyrics discussed here. For one thing, the new topic of choice for the post-Conquest lyric is quite a bit more familiar to us than the topics of the Anglo-Saxons. Eros in all its many aspects not only dominated the lyric genre, but even colored the tone and style of lyrics on the second most popular topic, Christian devotion. But in addition to the odd quirk of history that has kept eros in vogue in Western culture for almost a millennium now, post-conquest English lyrics are more accessible to us because their speakers had become more recognizable. First-person pronouns were now de rigueur, and the antecedents of all these *I*'s are manifest to modern readers partly because our lyric conventions have changed so little since the fourteenth century and partly because the conventions had by this time collapsed the choice of speaker to two. Although there are certainly exceptions, the personal and the fictive speakers were the two to have survived the replacement of the old topics with the new topic—in other words, to have survived the introduction of the courtly love lyric. Of course, adoptable speakers were and are still quite familiar to post-Conquest churchgoers (as in "The Lord is my shepherd"), to senders and receivers of greeting cards (as in "You are so many things to me,/ Lover, wife, and friend . . ." and to juvenile jumpers of rope (as in "A, my name is Alice"), and inanimate speakers were and are still familiar to children of all literacy levels, but lyric poetry composed for most adult audiences today eschews the inanimate and adoptable speakers just as surely as it does the nonpersonal speaker. The reasons for the demise of these kinds of speakers with the introduction of the courtly love lyric are obvious, as are the reasons that these speakers have remained out of fashion with the modern shift of preferred lyric topic from eros to other varieties of self-absorption. Despite this essential stasis in the Western lyric since the courtly love revolution of the twelfth century, one thing new is the current conflation of the fictive and personal speakers. The history of the relationship between fiction and biography / autobiography is a complex and fascinating one, but suffice it to say here that nowadays these categories have run together and many readers would say that there is no such thing at all as a personal speaker, since all speakers are fictive constructs of the poet. At any rate, readers of lyric poems of the High Middle Ages were on firmer ground than we in distinguishing between the personal speaker of, say, a complaint to the poet's patron, and the fictive coy shepherdess who speaks a pastoral love lyric written by a male poet.

The Normans, of course, cannot take the credit (or, perhaps, blame) for this change of conventions. Old English poetry, both lyric and narrative, was already stagnating when Edward the Confessor began to introduce his Norman friends and relatives into the English court, and we can imagine that an English England would have provided fertile ground for the seeds of the new lyric that were soon to be disseminated in all directions from Provence. Guillaume IX, the first known troubador, was born five years after the Battle of Hastings and the lyric style that he created (or of which he was an early representative) took less than a hundred years to flower in a culture that shared not a little with that of the Anglo-Saxons. I am referring, of course, to the great Middle High German lyrics of der von Kurenberc, Heinrich von Morungen, Reinmar von Hagenau, and Walther von der Vogelweide, all composed between 1150 and 1230. The existence of the German lyrics makes it clear that the political connection with southern France with which the Normans provided the English was scarcely necessary to introduce the new lyric style. The new literature would have made its way sooner or later to an English England just as surely as it made its way (much later) to an Icelandic Iceland.

The narrowing of topic and speakers and the consequent great flourishing of the European lyric has more to do with the development of the notion of the individual and the changes in the nature of literacy that accompanied that development. Communal settings for the reading aloud of lyric poetry from large manuscript books were gradually replaced by the individual, silent reading in a private room or even out of doors—a quintessentially Romantic activity. Poems that would previously have been circulated unsigned because no one had yet thought to take credit for his efforts within the tradition came gradually to be signed. The notion of authorship introduced or encouraged the notion that a poem one published is a static object, a piece of property labeled with the name of its creator. Both the shift to private reading and the introduction of the notion of authorship suggest a consequent preference for the individual speaker, whether it be the poet herself as a unique individual or a particular fictive persona through whom the poet can confront situations unavailable to himself. In any case, the early manuscript culture of the Anglo-Saxons, as preserved in its vernacular verse, with its craft literacy, marginally oral poetry, and democratic notions of the generation of a poem, came abruptly to an end with the Norman Conquest and thus the poems remain for us cut off from Western literary history at both ends. The old joke that Old English literature is a small body of poetry completely surrounded by scholars is in this sense true. It seems to me, though, that despite the Old English lyric's historical isolation (and the very formidable language barrier), as an artifact of human artistic impulse its appeal is universal. Old English lyrics can still occur for the modern reader for one of the very same reasons that they feel so alien: those unfamiliar and often scarcely human speakers who yet wondrously communicate with us and invite us to recognize them as subjects in their own right.

Notes

Chapter 1. Meanwhile, a Millennium Later . . .

1. See, for example, Cross on the *consolatio,* Woolf *("Wanderer")* on the *planctus,* Howlett ("Two") on the *encomium,* and Henry *(Early English)* on penitential poetry. The standard work on the *Frauenlied* is Frings, but A. Davidson's discussion is also excellent, as is Renoir's "Reading Context," which provides a valuable summary of women characters in Germanic literature.

2. Greenfield ("OE Elegies") and Shippey (53) authoritatively count only the first listed seven as elegies. See Timmer for a convincing argument for including only "Wulf" and "The Wife's Lament," and Renoir ("The Least Elegiac") for some well-taken doubts that any Old English poems qualify as elegies. Green, in his introduction to his recent edition of critical essays on the elegies, provides a handy discussion of some of the problems with the term "elegy," but concludes that the term is more useful than troublesome. Goldman redefines the Old English elegies as "laments for the living" (74), which accurately describes the five lyrics he discusses but which further narrows the genre.

3. Magoun and Creed (who limits his arguments to *Beowulf*) are the chief proponents of the oral-formulaic theory. See Creed (97 n.1) for further references. For arguments against the oral-formulaic theory and for lettered composition, see (in addition to Benson, Finnegan, and Stevik) Schaar, Watts, and Fry ("Memory"). Benson makes a particularly strong case for the lettered composition of Old English literature as a whole, as does Kiernan *(Beowulf)* for *Beowulf.*

4. Only two extant poems are explicitly spoken by *scops*: "Widsith," a mnemonic poem that probably is at least in part a transcription of orally preserved material, and "Deor," which was certainly composed pen-in-hand.

5. Cotton Vitellius A.xv, the book containing *Beowulf* and *Judith,* is much more manageable at about $9'' \times 6''$, and was more likely to have been intended for private reading than the Exeter Book, which contains so many of the lyrics discussed here.

6. Ruth Finnegan points out that some oral societies have clear and rigid notions of the ownership of poems, and gives examples of buying, inheriting, and using poems as gifts (203–4). The latter case is familiar from the Icelandic saga— one thinks of Egil's "Head Ransom," for example—but I know of no evidence for similar notions of ownership in Anglo-Saxon England.

7. Derek Pearsall cautions against resisting this conclusion: "Anglo-Saxon poetry, in its existing written form, is the product of monastic culture, and if our sense of the secular and heroic content of *Beowulf* [or any of the lyric poems, I would like to add, such as "The Battle of Brunanburh" or "Wulf and Eadwacer"] is so strong as to make us wish to resist such a conclusion, then probably what needs revising is not our sense of the poem but our concept of monastic culture" (19).

8. The quotation is from Wrenn (92). To my knowledge, the only modern critic

to suggest female authorship of any Old English poem is Clifford Davidson, who, in a 1975 article, writes that the author of "The Wife's Lament" "could indeed have been a woman" (457).

9. The nonexistence of the notion of selfhood in early manuscript cultures of course differs from Keats's concept of Negative Capability, which posits the consciousness of self in ordinary persons, but an obliteration of that self in great poets before they can compose. In contrast to both these notions is recent critical theory (e.g., Eco, Iser, and Fish) which posits the obliteration of the author's ego when the text is read. However, although neither of these modern notions (Keats's Negative Capability or the reader-focused critical theory of the 1980s) explicitly addresses the special problems of reading radically anonymous poems, they do prove helpful to the reader who finds no author in the text she reads.

Chapter 2. The Inanimate Speaker

1. The bishop is identified as Wulfstan, but since this name is written over an erasure, and since there was no bishop by the name of Wulfstan in Alfred's life time, this name is usually taken to be a mistake for Waerferth, the translator, although there have been other proposals. Keller (6–8 and 92–93) argues that Waerferth is intended, and that the poem belongs to the original of Waerferth's translation. Cook ("Unsuspected Bit") concurs, but the *ASPR* (6, cxvi–vii) and Sisam (*Studies* 201–3) each present complex arguments that Waerferth was not intended.

2. See Stewart (129 ff) on this point.

3. Williamson's *A Feast of Creatures* is the best discussion of the entire corpus, and each of his translations is a small masterpiece. Another good source, with more literal translations, is Baum's *Anglo-Saxon Riddles of the Exeter Book*.

4. Adams, in "The Anglo-Saxon Riddle as Lyric Mode," finds the riddles to be the only lyrical poems in Old English. In addition to Williamson and Adams, two other good discussions of the riddles as metaphors and/or lyric poems are Nelson's "Paradox of Silent Speech" and Stewart's "Kenning and Riddle." Of course, it was Aristotle (*Rhetoric* 1405b) who gave us all the idea.

5. Williamson uses his own numbering of the riddles. I have substituted the *ASPR* numbers, which I use throughout, for the reader's convenience, although Williamson's divisions are more sensible.

6. For arguments supporting the *ASPR* separation of Riddle 60 from the "The Husband's Message," see E. Anderson (*"Husband's Message"* and "Voices") and Leslie ("Integrity"). Among those arguing for the inclusion of Riddle 60 are Blackburn, Elliott ("Runes in *HM*"), and Goldsmith ("Enigma").

7. For arguments positing a runestaff as speaker, see Page (101), Bouman (64–65), and most standard interpretations of the poem. Arguing for a human messenger are Greenfield ("Old English Elegies" 169–70 and *Interpretation* 151) and Swanton (*"Wife's Lament"* 286). E. Anderson (*"Husband's Message"* and "Voices") finds both these speakers alternately. Goldsmith ("Enigma") was the first to suggest the reed pen as speaker.

8. The *ASPR* reading *gecyre* 'replace' is altogether uncertain: Goldsmith, the most recent scholar to have published the results of her inspection of the manuscript, favors *gehyre* 'hear' ("Enigma" 251). For other discussions of this word, see Bouman (70), Leslie (*Three* 66), Kaske (44), Orton ("Speaker" 50), and the *ASPR* note on this line, which also provides further bibliography on the question. It is not

clear whether the runes spell a word or whether they are to be read for their name values. If the former, there are only two plausible words to be formed from ᚻ [S], ᚱ [R], ᛇ [EA], ᚹ [W], and ᛞ [D or M: this rune is ambiguous, but most scholars take it to be the M rune]: *sweard* 'skin,' proposed by J. Anderson and glossed 'vellum' ("Deutungsmöglichkeiten"), and *smearw,* proposed by Bolton and glossed as *oleum (*"Wife's Lament" 340). Unfortunately, J. Anderson's gloss is simply not persuasive, and Bolton's proposal depends on a complex reading of the poem as an englishing of the Song of Songs. See Bouman (72) and the *ASPR* note on lines 49–50 for other solutions. If, on the other hand, the runes are to be read for their name values, as recent scholars almost unanimously agree, then we must form a sentence with the words *sigel* "sun," or *segl* "sail" as Peter Nicholson has recently proposed, *rad* "path," *ear* "earth" or "ocean", *wynn* "joy," and either *dæg* "day" or *mann* "man," which task is scarcely less formidable since it is hard to understand how the recipient could have made sense of this, let alone the Anglo-Saxon reader for whom the message was ultimately intended. Elliott ("Runes in HM" 7) interprets: "Follow the sun's path across the sea to find joy with the man who is waiting for you." Leslie (*Three* 17) interprets: "I hear heaven, earth, and the man declare together." P. Nicholson's interpretation of ᚻ as *segl* "sail" makes good sense in the compound *seglrad* "sail-path" or "sea."

9. For allegorical readings, see Kaske, Swanton (*"Wife's Lament"*), and Goldsmith ("Enigma").

Chapter 3. The Adoptable Speaker

1. Frazer established this distinction in *The Golden Bough.* See especially page 56.

2. Thus Duckert. Boenig provides a summary of the various interpretations of *erce* (139, n. 1).

3. See Tupper ("Notes") for further discussion.

Chapter 4. The Nonpersonal Speaker

1. The definition is from C. Hugh Holman, *A Handbook to Literature,* 4th ed. (Indianapolis: Bobbs-Merrill, 1972), s.v. 'hymn.'

2. Huppé, the major commentator on the "Hymn," does consider the poem a good paraphrase of Genesis (*Doctrine* 108).

3. See Schlauch ("Old English") for the idea that "Durham" is a school-boy exercise, and for the pertinent section of the *Translatio.*

4. See Campbell (35) and Klaeber ("Note" 7).

5. For a discussion of this device, see Bartlett (23) and Henry ("Celtic-English" passim).

6. For a different view of the structure, but a similar proposal for the title, see Isaacs (89–93).

7. Van't Hul and Mitchell have recently identified the poem's "earn æften hwit" as the white-tailed eagle, but this identification had already been made by Goldsmith in her 1954 article on "*The Seafarer* and the Birds" (234).

8. Isaacs discusses many of these same points (ch. 8) in what he calls "backward and forward movement" (122).

9. For example, Lipp (168) and Isaacs (118).

10. For arguments that "The Ruin" is not an elegy, see Howlett ("Two"), Timmer, and Keenan (114).

11. For arguments that the poem describes an actual ruin, see especially Hotchner, Wrenn (154), and Leslie (*Three* 29–30). Most modern scholars accept Hotchner's identification of the ruin as Bath, although Dunleavy suggests Chester and Herben suggests Hadrian's Wall. Hotchner proposes 775 as the *terminus ad quem* for the poem's composition (91), Leslie proposes 750 (26–28), and Kershaw, 676 (53, n. 10). For allegorical interpretations, see W. Johnson ("Ruin") and Keenan.

12. Leslie, however, sees a moving speaker: "From line 18, and perhaps before, the poet has been wandering among the ruins, recording what he saw as he went" (*Three* 29). It is difficult to see how Leslie gets this impression, since from line 18 through the end, the poem is almost entirely in the visionary past.

13. See Leslie (28). It is now generally accepted that this phrase is a reference to Doomsday.

14. Calder ("Perspective") and Anne T. Lee both have similar discussions of the role of time in "The Ruin."

15. Greenfield, for example, says that the poet "presents his picture detachedly and disinterestedly" (*Critical* 215), which is almost verbatim for Leslie's earlier statement that "the tone of the poet is detached and disinterested" (*Three* 30). Anne T. Lee points out that the expressions "þæt wæs hyðelic" and "þæt is cynelic þing" are "as close as he comes to making a personal comment of any kind" (453) and Hume notes "the absence of personal grief" (353).

16. This and all other quotations from *Beowulf* are from Klaeber's edition.

Chapter 5. The Fictive Speaker

1. Anacoluthic use of the personal pronouns is not peculiar to the fictive speakers, of course. Henry (*Early* 168) points out the following example from Alfred's translation of the *Pastoral Care:* "Ælfred kyning hateð gretan Wæferð biscep his wordum luflice ond freondlice; ond ðe cyðan hate ðæt me com swiðe oft on gemynd" [King Alfred greets Bishop Wæferth with his loving and friendly words, and I let it be known to you that it very often comes to my mind]. Such anacoluthon also occurs in "The Penitent's Prayer," "A Kentish Hymn," and Cynewulf's lyric epilogues.

2. Early scholars looked for a narrative background from the Germanic saga cycles, proposing the *Volsungasaga,* the Wolfdietrich B legend, and the Odoaker cycle (see Bouman 96 or *ASPR* 3:lvi for summaries), while two recent readings (Bouman 97–100 and Frankis) propose a connection with "Deor." None of these readings is convincing, if only because the poem lacks sufficient background narrative to allow us to make even a tentative identification of the story. Figurative readings have produced theories positing the poem as a charm (Fry "*Wulf*") and as a private note from a poet to his colleague or scribe protesting the mishandling of a poem (Eliason "On *Wulf*), both of which leave many obscurities unanswered. An early effort to read the poem literally on internal evidence alone was that of Sedgefield, who understood it as the dream of a female dog concerning her relationship with a wolf. This suggestion did have the virtue of explaining the names Wulf and Eadwacer, the latter an appropriate name for a watchdog, but it has never been taken seriously. More plausible explanations are those of Whitbread, who believes the situation to be a feud between the tribes of the speaker and of Wulf; of Adams ("*Wulf*"), who sees Wulf as a member of a group

something like the Holmsvikings, who proscribed women from their compound and allowed members out for only three days at a time; and Keough, who, in a thoughtful and valuable essay on the poem, sees Wulf as an outlaw, and the poem's theme as the personal and societal consequences of the separation of an outlaw from a society. Most recently, Osborn ("Text") and Frese ("*Wulf*") have suggested independently that Wulf is not the speaker's lover, but rather her son. Both Osborn and Frese work under the assumption that a woman's love for her son is a more typical Anglo-Saxon literary theme than is a woman's love for her husband or lover, and this is certainly true of the extant literature, and probably true of the literature as a whole. Nevertheless, it seems to me unlikely, no matter how typical, that a mother's grief for her prodigal (according to Osborn) or dead (according to Frese) son is the theme of this particular poem. The final lines imply illicit sexual love between the speaker and Wulf, an implication on which both Osborn and Frese are silent. Furthermore, Osborn offers almost no support for her reading, and Frese's voluminous evidence, taken from runic Norse inscription, is mostly in-analogous.

3. Until 1969, when Lehmann ("Metrics") reintroduced the idea, Lawrence ("First Riddle") had been the last major critic to see "Wulf" as a fragment. Lawrence thought the lacuna fell between lines 1 and 2, but Lehmann suggests that the missing lines precede the text as we have it. Both base their conjectures on the poem's metrics, rather than on the sense and structure.

4. Frankis (173), Keough (558), and Spamer (144) concur.

5. The uncertainty of this line is caused by the fact that in the manuscript, *her* ends one line and *heard* begins the next, making it impossible to tell for sure where or if word division was intended. Thus, we may read the line "Het mec hlaford min (herh-eard/her heard) niman" as either "My lord bade me occupy a grove dwelling (i.e., pagan sanctuary)" or "My cruel lord bade me betake myself here." Obviously, how we read this line bears greatly on how we understand both the setting and of the speaker's relationship to her husband.

6. For interpretations of the husband as a sympathetic figure, see especially Ward, Leslie (*Three*), Davis, Curry, Rissanen, and L. Johnson. Bouman also finds the lord a sympathetic figure, but he posits a second, cruel husband (60). Greenfield, in an argument he later retracted ("*Wife's Lament*") and Lench posit a hostile husband, Lench understanding him to be the speaker's murderer. Doane suggests that the speaker is a pagan deity abandoned by her recently Christianized priest, but this view is hard to reconcile with the speaker's apparent subordination to the lord.

7. Wentersdorf attempts to explain that the setting is a pagan sanctuary, and thus a logical place for an Anglo-Saxon in trouble to take up temporary residence. Despite voluminous external evidence, the internal evidence is insufficient. Lench's reading, which finds the speaker to be a revenant, of course is free from such concerns. Tripp also posits a revenant as speaker in a figurative reading that posits the lord as the rational soul and the speaker as "the animal soul in the body, the revenant yearning for the "hope of the world," the pleasure it once knew of being alive" (358). Of this figurative reading one can say only that there is no hint in our text of the poem that this is so.

8. The strong possibility that the speaker of "The Wife's Lament" is a literary or folktale character whose situation would have been well known to the poem's Anglo-Saxon readership has not received much attention recently, perhaps because earlier scholars have exhausted the sources available to us. Among the sources or analogues for "The Wife's Lament" are the Offa saga (a variant on the

Constance tale), the Odoaker saga, the Crescentia tale, and the Old Irish "Liadain and Curither" (all summarized in Leslie *Three* 9–10), and more recently, the folktale "The Search for the Lost Husband" (Fitzgerald). The idea that "The Wife's Lament" is an allusion to a folktale or narrative poem seems probable in light of the wealth of detail, most of it incomprehensible, that the poem presents, but all this detail has proven not quite enough to show any definite connection between the poem and any of these possible sources.

9.   Swanton was the first to suggest an allegorical reading, positing the idea that the poem was based on the two exegetical images of "The Journey of Life and Death," and "The Heavenly Bride" (*"Wife's Lament"* 275). In this he was followed by Bolton (*"Wife's Lament"*), who further found the poem to be an englishing of the Song of Songs. Both Swanton and Bolton depend upon the reader's acceptance of a connection between "The Wife's Lament" and "The Husband's Message." If this connection is not accepted, and there seems no good reason why it should be, then the arguments lose much of their strength. The same can be said of Kaske's suggestion that the poem is "a lament by the divorced and abandoned Synagogue," made in a note to his essay on "The Husband's Message" (71, n. 81). (Howlett, in *"Wife's Lament,"* attempts to show a connection between the two poems on formal evidence, and is the only one of these four scholars to argue without begging the question.) One problem, but a significant one, with all these figurative readings is that they ignore the indications in the poem that the lord and his kinsmen have acted less than fairly with respect to the speaker, a situation that is incompatible with understanding the lord to be Christ, the Church, or the rational soul (as does Tripp).

10.   Henry establishes its gnomic intent with a lexical study (*Early English* 101); Greenfield has since retracted his suggestion that it is a curse ("OE Elegies" 168); and Wentersdorf calls it "demonstrably gnomic" (515).

11.   W. Johnson (*"Wife's Lament"*) reads the poem as a Germanic death song.

12.   Although Eliason's theory brings up a number of important points about the relationship of the poet to his persona and his material, it is ultimately unconvincing, for among other shortcomings it does not explain why such an occasional poem would have been written down and included in the Exeter Book.

13.   Lawrence asks, "Is it not perfectly clear that we are dealing with an imaginary situation, not with actual fact?" ("Song" 21), and more recent scholars declare: "This tale of the poet's own trouble is to be regarded as fictitious" (Malone, *Deor* 16); "The vatic 'ic' of the poem . . . is no more literal than the [allegorical figures of Boethius]" (Bolton, "Boethius" 226); "The poem is a dramatic monologue" (Frankis 165); and "Deor [is] a fictitious speaker-poet" (Greenfield, *Critical History* 161).

14.   See Malone *(Deor),* Isaacs (107–8), and Wrenn (83) to this effect.

15.   On the pronoun referent in the repeated line, see Greenfield (*Critical History* 160), Malone (*Deor* 17), Mandel (1), and Shippey (75). J. Anderson suggests a different interpretation of the repeated line in connection with his essay on the unity of "Deor" and "Wulf": translating as "That was moved on, so can this be, too," he suggests that the first pronoun refers to the immediately preceding story and the second to the immediately following story, which in the last instance is the poem "Wulf" (*"Deor"* 206). On the nature of the misfortune, see Mandel (passim) and Frankis (171–72). For Boethian interpretations, see Bolton ("Boehius"), Kiernan (*"Deor"*), and Markland.

16.   J. Anderson has recently proposed a similar connection ("Deor"). Unfortunately, both Frankis's and J. Anderson's essays are rendered unconvincing by a great deal of question begging.

17. This second possibility is suggested by Tuggle (235), but most other scholars follow Malone (8–9) in understanding the passage to refer to the Orpheus-figure Gaut. J. Anderson suggests yet another narrative: the story of Hild and Heoden ("*Deor*" 210).

18. O. S. Anderson (who later writes under the name Arngart), in a seminal 1937 monograph on "The Seafarer," provides a good summary of opinion on the question of the speaker up to that date. At that time, the consensus of the nineteenth-century German philologists that the poem was a dialogue had been effectively exploded by Lawrence ("*Wanderer* and *Seafarer*") in 1902, and Anderson was able confidently to consider the poem as spoken by one man. However, the two-speaker theory has reappeared twice since Anderson's monograph, first in a 1956 essay by Stanley, who calls the speaker of lines 1–33a an "ethopoeic exile" and the speaker of the remaining lines (who quotes the first) "the wise, pious man eager to go on a pilgrimage" (454), and then again in Pope's 1965 essay on "dramatic Voices in *The Wanderer* and *The Seafarer*," in which Pope posited not only two ethopoeic speakers, but a poet's voice as well in the epilogue.

The question of the number of speakers in the poem centers chiefly on a single word, *sylf*, in 35a. If *sylf* is taken to mean "myself," then a second speaker is implied, but *sylf* has also been understood as meaning "of my own accord," "for myself," and "by myself, alone." Greenfield and Pope have each written two essays on the speaker question and the meaning of *sylf*, and each retracts his first reading in his second essay. To follow this vexed question, read, in the order given, Pope, "Dramatic Voices"; Greenfield, "*Min, Sylf*, and 'Dramatic Voices' "; Pope, "Second Thoughts"; and Greenfield, "*Sylf*, Seasons." Since Pope retracted his dialogue theory in 1974 ("Second Thoughts"), it has now no serious defenders. It seems clear that there is no good reason for positing a second speaker at 33b.

19. Among allegorical interpretations, O. S. Anderson's was the first to present a detailed reading of the poem as an allegory, although he credits Gustav Ehrismann with the idea (9). Anderson's reading takes the difficult voyage up through 33a to represent the poet's life, and the longed for voyage across the high seas in 33b ff to represent his journey to heaven. See also Smithers. Others, including Anderson himself writing more than forty years later, have shied away from the designation "allegory," preferring to call the seafaring an "imagined situation" (Stanley 453), a symbol (Gordon 8), a "symbolic depiction" (Alvin A. Lee 144), a metaphor (Vickrey), "a journey traveled metaphorically" (Shields 37), a parable (Arngart, 252), or an *exemplum* (Osborn "Venturing" 4 and Arngart). Tripp also calls the seafaring section an exemplum, interpreting this poem as the utterance of a revenant. In defending his hypothesis, which he also applies to "The Wanderer" and "The Wife's Lament," he calls our attention to a great deal of death imagery in these lyrics and his essay is valuable in this, but it has thus far failed to convince any other commentator on the poem. Regardless of the differences in critical terminology, it is clear that the seafaring section is a concrete figuration of the abstract topic of the poem.

20. Whitelock ("Interpretation") holds that the poem is the monologue of an actual *peregrinus,* a pilgrim or voluntary exile, a figure that, from Whitelock's sources, appears to have been common during the Anglo-Saxon period. Henry provides further support for Whitelock's theory with many more examples of the *peregrinus* tradition in England and Ireland (*Early English* 35–39), and Leslie ("Meaning and Structure") has recently made use of this interpretation to point out that the literal exile helps the reader to recognize the metaphoric exile that Leslie also finds in the poem.

Chapter 6. The Personal Speaker

1. The uncertainties that modern scholars find in interpreting the runes are not discussed in the text of this study since the general sense and the tone of the passages are not greatly affected by the variants on the rune names: a brief summary of the situation is given here for reference. The problem in interpreting these passages is that we do not, and cannot, know for certain what name value each rune had for Cynewulf and his audience. The name values given in the Old English "Rune Poem" do not in all cases match the name values of the runes in other Germanic languages, nor do they all make sense in Cynewulf's epilogues. We can be fairly certain in assigning name values to five of the runes whose names are common OE words: ᚾ *nyd* (need); ᛗ *eoh* (horse); ᛈ *wynn* (joy); ᛚ *lagu* (water); and ᚠ *feoh* "wealth." The names of the remaining three as given in the "Rune Poem," however, do not appear elsewhere in OE and do not seem to most scholars to be appropriate in the context of the epilogues. These three are ᚻ *cen* (torch); ᛇ *yr* (bow); and ᚢ *ur* "bison." Most scholars assign them alternate name values: *cene* (bold) or (the bold one) for *cen; yrre* (wrathful), *yrmþu* (wretchedness) or *yfel* (evil) for *yr;* and *ure* (our) for *ur*. For complete discussions on these variants, see Brown (206–8), Kennedy (*Earliest* 362–63), Page (206), Shippey (157), and Tupper ("Cynewulfian" passim). However, Elliott ("Cynewulf's Runes" passim) and Frese ("Art" 313) have argued for retaining the name values given in the "Rune Poem" on the grounds that there is no evidence for any of these alternate values and that the runic signature would not have been comprehensible to Cynewulf's audience if the name values were not fixed. While it is probably true that Cynewulf understood the name values as fixed, it does not necessarily follow that they matched those given in the "Rune Poem," which may date from a different period, or may be eccentric or influenced by Scandinavian tradition. In light of the inconclusiveness of all these interpretations, it seems best to resign oneself to uncertainty in this matter unless new information becomes available. It should be pointed out here, too, that the use of runes seems to have been conventionally associated with Christian prayer formulas. For examples, see Elliott (*Runes* 84–97).

2. Early scholars thought the epilogues to be autobiographical, stating that they give the reader "insight into [Cynewulf's] character" (Kennedy *Poems* 198) or that they show him to have been "addicted to personal revelations" (Cook *Dream* xxxix); most readers today agree that the "autobiographical" material in the epilogues is conventional. See, for example, Brown (217–19), Calder (*Cynewulf* 140), Greenfield (*Critical History* 108), and E. Anderson (*Cynewulf* 18).

3. E. Anderson goes even further in emphasizing the communal aspect of this poem, finding evidence in the first-person plural pronouns and in the repeated verb *gehyrdon* that "Fates" was composed in the social context of group lections in the monastery (*Cynewulf* 19, 81).

4. The expression "gamelum to geoce" (1248a) is usually taken to mean that Cynewulf received the gift in his old age, but as Brown points out (220), it may mean that the gift, whenever acquired, proved of special help in Cynewulf's later years.

Chapter 7. Two Masterpieces

1. The shifts in style, topic, and speaker at these lines are regularly mentioned by critics of the poem. Pasternack has a brief summary of scholarly opinion as well as an interesting analysis of the stylistic disjunctions at these lines.

2. This inscription runs around the edges of the cross. A second inscription, on the arms, reads: "Drahmal me worhte" [Drahmal made me]. It is interesting to notice that aside from this signature, the text proper is in verse when it is spoken by the reliquary and in prose when it is in the third person. Perhaps Drahmal (the name looks like a Norse cognomen) instinctively felt that prosopopoeia goes with verse, both belonging to the oral tradition and to the tradition of runic inscriptions, and not with prose, which is not written until literacy is well established. The inscription is in Roman characters, however.

3. See, for example, Dickens and Ross (17–18), *ASPR* 6, cxxii, and Stevik (passim).

4. See Orton ("Technique") for a discussion of methods of object personification, including similarities between the "Dream" and the riddles.

5. For interpretations in which this distance is understood as prescribed in some way or another by Christian doctrine, see Woolf ("Doctrinal Influences"), Payne, and Burlin.

6. Edwards, in an essay on narrative technique and distancing in "The Dream," reaches a similar conclusion, albeit by a different route, and likewise finds that the poem has to do with human perception rather than the Crucifixion.

7. Richman's recent article on these three clauses shows persuasively that "on mode" is to be construed with "cwæð" rather than with "snottor."

8. Among those who hold this view, see especially Lawrence ("*Wanderer*"), Lumiansky, Greenfield ("Old English Elegies" 147 and *Critical History* 217), and Dunning and Bliss's introduction to their edition. The one Old English lyric that assuredly does have this Chinese box structure, "The Dream of the Rood," is quite explicit in designating its speakers, and so offers no support for this reading of "The Wanderer."

9. For a strictly realistic reading of the wanderer's situation, see Elliott ("The Wanderer's Conscience").

10. Rosier (366, n.2) was the first to point out the concentration of words having to do with mind: thirty-five in all. Calder discusses the ramifications of this diction in his valuable essay on the poem ("Setting and Mode"). See also Shippey's discussion of "The Wanderer," 56 ff, especially p. 67.

Works Cited

Adams, John F. "The Anglo-Saxon Riddle as Lyric Mode." *Criticism* 7 (1965): 335–48.

———. "*Wulf and Eadwacer:* An Interpretation." *Modern Language Notes* 73 (1958): 1–5.

Albertson, Clinton, S. J., trans. *Anglo-Saxon Saints and Heroes.* New York: Fordham University Press, 1967.

Albright, Daniel. *Lyricality in English Literature.* Lincoln: University of Nebraska Press, 1985.

Anderson, Earl R. *Cynewulf: Structure, Style, and Theme in His Poetry.* London: Associated University Presses, 1983.

———. "*The Husband's Message:* Persuasion and the Problem of *Genyre.*" *English Studies* 56 (1975): 289–94.

———. "Voices in *The Husband's Message.*" *Neuphilologische Mitteilungen* 74 (1973): 238–46.

Anderson, James E. "*Deor, Wulf and Eadwacer,* and *The Soul's Address:* How and Where the Old English Exeter Book Riddles Begin." In *The Old English Elegies: New Essays in Criticism and Research,* edited by Martin Green, 204–30.

———. "Die Deutungsmöglichkeiten des altenglischen Gedichtes *The Husband's Message.*" *Neuphilologische Mitteilungen* 75 (1974): 402–7.

Anderson, O. S. "*The Seafarer": An Interpretation.* Lund: K. Humanistika Vetenskapssamfundets i Lund Arsberattelse I, 1937–38.

Aristotle. *Rhetoric. Rhetoric and Poetics,* translated by W. Rhys Roberts. New York: Modern Library-Random, 1954.

Arngart, O. "*The Seafarer:* A Postscript." *English Studies* 60 (1979): 249–53.

Asser. *Life of Alfred.* In *Alfred the Great: Asser's Life of Alfred and Other Contemporary Sources,* translated and edited by Simon Keynes and Michael Lapidge. Middlesex, UK: Penguin, 1983.

Bäuml, Franz H. "Varieties and Consequences of Medieval Literacy and Illiteracy." *Speculum* 55 (1980): 237–65.

Barthes, Roland. "Literature and Discontinuity." In *Critical Essays,* translated by Richard Howard, 171–83. Evanston, IL: Northwestern University Press, 1972.

Bartlett, Adeline Courtney. *The Larger Rhetorical Patterns in Anglo-Saxon Poetry.* Morningside Heights, New York: Columbia University Press, 1935.

Baum, Paull F. *Anglo-Saxon Riddles of the Exeter Book.* Durham, NC: Duke University Press, 1963.

Bede. *A History of the English Church and People,* translated by Leo Sherley-Price. Rev. R. E. Latham. Middlesex, UK: Penguin, 1968.

Benjamin, Walter. "The Work of Art in the Age of Mechanical Reproduction." In *Illuminations,* edited by Hannah Arendt. New York: Harcourt, 1955.

Benson, Larry D. "The Literary Character of Anglo-Saxon Formulaic Poetry." *PMLA* 81 (1966): 334–41.

Benveniste, Emile. *Problems in General Linguistics,* translated by M. E. Meek. Coral Gables, FL: University of Miami Press, 1971.

Blackburn, Francis A. "The *Husband's Message* and the Accompanying Riddles of the Exeter Book." *Journal of Germanic Philology* 3 (1901): 1–13.

Blake, Norman F. "The Dating of Old English Poetry." *An English Miscellany Presented to W. S. Mackie,* edited by Brian S. Lee, 14–27. London: Oxford University Press, 1977.

Bliss, Alan, and Allen J. Frantzen. "The Integrity of *Resignation.*" *Review of English Studies* 27 (1976): 387–402.

Bloomfield, Morton W. "The Form of *Deor.*" In *Old English Literature: Twenty-two Analytical Essays,* edited by Martin Stevens and Jerome Mandel, 212–28. Lincoln: University of Nebraska Press, 1968.

Boenig, Robert. "*Erce* and Dew." *Names* 31 (1983): 130–31.

Bolton, Whitney F. "Boethius, Alfred, and *Deor* Again." *Modern Philology* 69 (1971–72): 222–27.

———. "The Dimensions of *The Wanderer.*" *Leeds Studies in English* 3 (1969): 7–34.

———. "'Variation' in *The Battle of Brunanburh.*" *Review of English Studies* ns 19 (1968): 363–72.

———. "*The Wife's Lament* and *The Husband's Message:* A Reconsideration Revisited." *Archiv für das Studium der Neueren Sprachen und Literaturen* 201 (1969): 337–51.

Boren, James L. "The Design of the Old English *Deor.*" In *Anglo-Saxon Poetry: Essays in Appreciation,* edited by Lewis E. Nicholson and Dolores Warwick Frese, 264–76. Notre Dame, IN: University of Notre Dame Press, 1975.

Bouman, A. C. *Patterns in Old English and Old Icelandic Literature.* Leiden: Universitaire Pers, 1962.

Brown, Carleton. "The Autobiographical Element in the Cynewulfian Rune Passage." *Englische Studien* 38 (1907): 196–233.

Buber, Martin. *I and Thou,* translated by Walter Kaufmann. New York: Scribner's, 1970.

Burlin, Robert B. "The Ruthwell Cross, *The Dream of the Rood,* and the Vita Contemplativa." *Studies in Philology* 65 (1968): 23–43.

Calder, Daniel G. *Cynewulf.* Boston: Twayne, 1981.

———. "Perspective and Movement in *The Ruin.*" *Neuphilologische Mitteilungen* 72 (1971): 442–45.

———. "Setting and Mode in *The Seafarer* and *The Wanderer.*" *Neuphilologische Mitteilungen* 72 (1971): 264–75.

Campbell, Alistair, ed. *The Battle of Brunanburh.* London: Heinemann, 1938.

Clanchy, M. T. *From Memory to Written Record: England, 1066–1307.* Cambridge, MA: Harvard University Press, 1979.

Condren, Edward I. "'Deor's' Artistic Triumph." *Studies in Philology* 78.5 (1981): 62–76.

Cook, Albert S., ed. *The Dream of the Rood.* Oxford: Clarendon, 1905.

———. "An Unsuspected Bit of Old English Verse." *Modern Language Notes* 17.1 (1902): col. 14–20.

Creed, Robert P. "On the Possibility of Criticizing Old English Poetry." *Texas Studies in Literature & Language* 3 (1961): 97–106.

Cross, J. E. "On the Genre of *The Wanderer.*" *Neophilologus* 45 (1961): 63–75.

Curry, Jane L. "Approaches to a Translation of the Anglo-Saxon *The Wife's Lament.*" *Medium Ævum* 35 (1966): 187–98.

Davidson, Arnold E. "Interpreting *Wulf and Eadwacer.*" *Annuale Mediaevale* 16 (1975): 24–32.

Davidson, Clifford. "Erotic 'Women's Songs' in Anglo-Saxon England." *Neophilologus* 59 (1975): 451–62.

Davis, Thomas M. "Another View of 'The Wife's Lament.'" *Papers on English Language & Literature* 1 (1965): 291–305.

Dickens, Bruce, and Alan S. C. Ross, eds. *The Dream of the Rood.* London: Methuen, 1934.

Doane, A. N. "Heathen Form and Christian Function in 'The Wife's Lament.'" *Mediaeval Studies* 28 (1966): 77–91.

Dronke, Peter. *The Medieval Lyric.* London: Hutchinson, 1968.

Duckert, Audrey R. "*Erce* and Other Possibly Keltic Elements in the Old English Charm for Unfruitful Land." *Names* 20 (1972): 83–90.

Dunleavy, Gareth W. "A 'De Exidio' Tradition in the Old English Ruin?" *Philological Quarterly* 38 (1959): 112–18.

Dunning, T. P., and A. J. Bliss, eds. *The Wanderer.* London: Methuen, 1969.

Edwards, Robert R. "Narrative Technique and Distance in *The Dream of the Rood. Papers on Language & Literature* 61 (1970): 291–301.

Eliason, Norman E. "On *Wulf and Eadwacer.*" In *Old English Studies in Honor of John C. Pope,* edited by Robert B. Burlin and Edward B. Irving, 225–34. Toronto: University of Toronto Press, 1974.

———. "Two Old English Scop Poems." *PMLA* 81 (1966): 185–92.

Elliott, Ralph W. V. "Cynewulf's Runes in *Christ II* and *Elene.*" *English Studies* 34 (1953): 49–57.

———. "Cynewulf's Runes in *Juliana* and *Fates of the Apostles.*" *English Studies* 34 (1953): 193–204.

———. *Runes.* Manchester, U.K.: Manchester University Press, 1959.

———. "The Runes in *The Husband's Message.*" *Journal of English and Germanic Philology* 54 (1955): 1–8.

———. "The Wanderer's Conscience." *English Studies* 39 (1958): 193–200.

Fanagan, John M. "An Examination of Tense-Usage in Some of the Shorter Poems of *The Exeter Book.*" *Neophilologus* 62 (1978): 290–93.

Finnegan, Ruth. *Oral Poetry: Its Nature, Significance, and Social Context.* Cambridge: Cambridge University Press, 1977.

Fish, Stanley. *Is There a Text in This Class?: The Authority of Interpretive Communities.* Cambridge, MA: Harvard University Press, 1980.

Fitzgerald, Robert P. "*The Wife's Lament* and 'The Search for the Lost Husband.'" *Journal of English and Germanic Philology* 62 (1963): 769–77.

Foucault, Michel. "What Is An Author?" In *Language, Counter-Memory, Practice: Selected Essays and Interviews,* edited by Donald F. Bouchard, 113–38. Ithaca: Cornell University Press, 1977.

Frankis, P. J. "*Deor* and *Wulf and Eadwacer:* Some Conjectures." *Medium Ævum* 31 (1962): 161–75.

Frazer, James George. *The Golden Bough: A Study in Magic and Religion.* Abridged edition. New York: Macmillan, 1922.

Frese, Dolores Warwick. "The Art of Cynewulf's Runic Signatures." In *Anglo-Saxon Poetry: Essays in Appreciation,* edited by Lewis E. Nicholson and Dolores Warwick Frese, 312–34. Notre Dame, IN: University of Notre Dame Press, 1975.

———. "*Wulf and Eadwacer:* The Adulterous Woman Reconsidered." *Notre Dame English Journal* 15 (1983): 1–22.

Frings, Theodor. "Minnesinger und Troubadours." *Deutsche Akademie der Wissenschaften, Vortrag, und Schriften,* fasc. 34. Berlin: n. p., 1949.

Fry, Donald. "The Memory of Cædmon." In *Oral Traditional Literature,* edited by John Miles Foley, 282–93. Columbus, Ohio: Slavica, 1981.

———. "*Wulf and Eadwacer:* A Wen Charm." *The Critical Review* 5 (1971): 247–63.

Frye, Northrop. *Anatomy of Criticism.* Princeton, NJ: Princeton University Press, 1957.

Goldman, Stephen H. "The Use of Christian Belief in Old English Poems of Exile." *Res Publica Litterarum: Studies in the Classical Tradition* 2 (1979): 69–80.

Goldsmith, Margaret E. "The Enigma of *The Husband's Message.*" In *Anglo-Saxon Poetry: Essays in Appreciation,* edited by Nicholson and Frese, 242–63. Notre Dame, IN: University of Notre Dame Press, 1975.

———. "The Seafarer and the Birds." *Review of English Studies* 5 (1954): 225–35.

Gordon, I. L., ed. *The Seafarer.* London: Methuen, 1960.

Green, Martin. "Introduction." In *The Old English Elegies: New Essays in Criticism and Research,* edited by Martin Green, 11–28. Rutherford, NJ: Fairleigh Dickinson University Press, 1983.

———, ed. *The Old English Elegies: New Essays in Criticism and Research.* Rutherford, NJ: Fairleigh Dickinson University Press, 1983.

Greenfield, Stanley B. *A Critical History of Old English Literature.* New York: New York University Press, 1965.

———. *The Interpretation of Old English Poems.* London: Routledge, 1972.

———. "*Min, Sylf,* and 'Dramatic Voices in *The Wanderer* and *The Seafarer.*'" *Journal of English and Germanic Philology* 68 (1969): 212–20.

———. "The Old English Elegies." In *Continuations and Beginnings,* edited by Eric Gerald Stanley, 142–75. London: Nelson, 1966.

———. "*Sylf,* Seasons, Structure and Genre in *The Seafarer.*" *Anglo-Saxon England* 9 (1981): 199–211.

———. "*The Wife's Lament* Reconsidered." *PMLA* 68 (1953): 907–12.

Greenfield, Stanley B., and Daniel G. Calder. *A New Critical History of Old English Literature.* New York: New York University Press, 1986.

Havelock, Eric A. *The Literate Revolution in Greece and Its Cultural Consequences.* Princeton, NJ: Princeton University Press, 1982.

———. *The Muse Learns to Write.* New Haven, CT: Yale University Press, 1986.

Heidegger, Martin. "The Origin of the Work of Art." *Poetry, Language, Thought,* translated by Albert Hofstadter, 15–87. New York: Harper, 1971.

Henry, Patrick Leo. "A Celtic-English Prosodic Feature." *Zeitschrift für Celtische Philologie* 29 (1962): 91–99.

———. *The Early English and Celtic Lyric.* London: Allen, 1966.

Herben, Stephen J. "*The Ruin.*" *Modern Language Notes* 54 (1939): 37–39.

Hieatt, Constance B. "Dream Frame and Verbal Echo in *The Dream of the Rood.*" *Neuphilologische Mitteilungen English Studies* 72 (1971): 251–63.

Hotchner, Cecilia. *Wessex and Old English Poetry, with Special Consideration of* The Ruin. Lancaster: Lancaster, 1939.

Howlett, D. R. "Two Old English Encomia." *English Studies* 57 (1976): 289–93.

———. "*The Wife's Lament* and *The Husband's Message.*" *Neuphilologische Mitteilungen* 79 (1978): 7–10.

Hume, Kathryn. "The 'Ruin Motif' in Old English Poetry." *Anglia* 94 (1976): 339–60.

Huppé, Bernard F. "*The Wanderer:* Theme and Structure." *Journal of English and Germanic Philology* 42 (1943): 516–38.

———. *Doctrine and Poetry: Augustine's Influence on Old English Poetry.* N. p.: State University of New York Press, 1959.

Irving, Edward B., Jr. "Image and Meaning in the Elegies." In *Old English Poetry: Fifteen Essays,* edited by Robert P. Creed, 153–66. Providence: Brown University Press, 1967.

Isaacs, Neil D. *Structural Principles in Old English Poetry.* Knoxville: University of Tennessee Press, 1968.

Jakobson, Roman. "Closing Statement: Linguistics and Poetics." In *Style in Language,* edited by Thomas A. Sebeok, 350–77. Cambridge, MA: Technology Press of MIT, 1960.

Johnson, Lee Ann. "The Narrative Structure of 'The Wife's Lament.'" *English Studies* 52 (1971): 497–501.

Johnson, William C., Jr. "*The Ruin* as Body-City Riddle." *Philological Quarterly* 59 (1980): 397–411.

———. "*The Wife's Lament* as Death Song." In *The Old English Elegies: New Essays in Criticism and Research,* edited by Martin Green, 69–81. Rutherford: Fairleigh Dickinson University Press, 1938.

Kaske, Robert E. "A Poem of the Cross in the Exeter Book: 'Riddle 60' and 'The Husband's Message.'" *Traditio* 23 (1967): 41–71.

Keats, John. Letters. *English Romantic Writers,* edited by David Perkins, 1205–37. New York: Harcourt, 1967.

Keenan, Hugh T. "*The Ruin* as Babylon." *Tennessee Studies in Literature* 11 (1966): 109–17.

Keller, Wolfgang. *Die Litterarischen Bestrebungen von Worchester in ags Zeit.* Strassburg: Trubner, 1900.

Kennedy, Charles W. *The Earliest English Poetry.* London: Oxford University Press, 1943.

———. *The Poems of Cynewulf.* London: Routledge, 1910.

Keough, Terrence. "The Tension of Separation in *Wulf and Eadwacer.*" *Neuphilologische Mitteilungen* 77 (1976): 552–60.

Kershaw, Nora. *Anglo-Saxon and Norse Poems.* Cambridge: Cambridge University Press, 1922.

Kiernan, Kevin S. *Beowulf and the Beowulf Manuscript.* New Brunswick, NJ: Rutgers University Press, 1981.

———. *"Deor:* The Consolations of an Anglo-Saxon Boethius." *Neuphilologische Mitteilungen* 79 (1978): 33–40.

Klaeber, Fredrich. "A Note on the Battle of Brunanburh." In *Anglia: Untersuchen zur englischen Philologie,* 1–7. Leipzig: Mayer & Muller, 1925.

———, ed. *Beowulf and the Fight at Finnsburg.* 3rd ed. Lexington: Heath, 1950.

Krapp, George Philip, and Elliott Van Kirk Dobbie, eds. *The Anglo-Saxon Poetic Records: A Collective Edition.* New York: Columbia University Press, 1931–1942.

Lawrence, W. W. "The Banished Wife's Lament." *Modern Philology* 5 (1908): 387–405.

———. "The First Riddle of Cynewulf." *PMLA* 17 (1902): 247–61.

———. "The Song of Deor." *Modern Philology* 9 (1911): 7–23.

———. *"The Wanderer* and *The Seafarer." Journal of Germanic Philology* 4 (1902): 460–80.

Lee, Alvin A. *The Guest-Hall of Eden.* New Haven: Yale Universty Press, 1972.

Lee, Anne T. *"The Ruin:* Bath or Babylon? A Nonarchaeological Investigation." *Neuphilologische Mitteilungen* 74 (1973): 443–55.

Lehmann, Ruth P. M. "The Metrics and Structure of *Wulf and Eadwacer." Philological Quarterly* 48 (1969): 151–65.

———. "The Old English *Riming Poem:* Interpretation, Text, and Translation." *Journal of English and Germanic Philology* 69 (1970): 437–49.

Lench, Elinor. *"The Wife's Lament:* A Poem of the Living Dead." *Comitatus* 1 (1970): 3–23.

Leslie, R. F. "The Integrity of Riddle 60." *Journal of English and Germanic Philology* 67 (1968): 451–57.

———. "The Meaning and Structure of *The Seafarer."* In *Old English Elegies: New Essays in Criticism and Research,* edited by Martin Green, 96–122. Rutherford, NJ: Fairleigh Dickinson University Press, 1983.

———, ed. *Three Old English Elegies.* Manchester: Manchester University Press, 1961.

Lipp, Frances Randall. "Contrast and Point of View in *The Battle of Brunanburh." Philological Quarterly* 48 (1969): 166–77.

Lord, Albert B. *The Singer of Tales.* Cambridge: Harvard University Press, 1964.

Lumiansky, R. M. "The Dramatic Structure of the Old English *Wanderer." Neophilologus* 34 (1950): 104–12.

Macrae-Gibson, O. D., ed. *The Old English Riming Poem.* Cambridge: Brewer, 1983.

Magoun, Francis P., Jr. "The Oral Formulaic Character of Anglo-Saxon Narrative Poetry." *Speculum* 28 (1953): 446–67.

Malone, Kemp, ed. *Deor.* New York: Appleton, 1966.

———. "Two Old English *Frauenlieder." Comparative Literature* 14 (1962): 106–17.

Mandel, Jerome. "Exemplum and Refrain: The Meaning of *Deor.*" *Yearbook of English Studies* 7 (1977): 1–9.

Markland, Murray F. "Boethius, Alfred, and *Deor.*" *Modern Philology* 66 (1968–69): 1–4.

Nelson, Marie. "The Paradox of Silent Speech in the Exeter Book Riddles." *Neophilologus* 62 (1978): 609–15.

Nicholson, Lewis E., and Dolores Warwick Frese, eds. *Anglo-Saxon Poetry: Essays in Appreciation.* Notre Dame, IN: University of Notre Dame Press, 1975.

Nicholson, Peter. "The Old English Rune for *S.*" *Journal of English and Germanic Philology* 81 (1982): 313–19.

Ong, Walter. *Orality and Literacy.* London: Methuen, 1982.

Orton, Peter. "The Speaker in *The Husband's Message.*" *Leeds Studies in English* 12 (1981): 43–56.

———. "The Technique of Object-Personification in *The Dream of the Rood* and a Comparison with the Old English Riddles." *Leeds Studies in English* 11 (1980): 1–18.

Osborn, Marijane. "The Text and Context of *Wulf and Eadwacer.*" In *The Old English Elegies: New Essays in Appreciation and Research,* edited by Martin Green, 174–89. Rutherford, NJ: Fairleigh Dickinson University Press, 1983.

———. "Venturing upon Deep Waters in *The Seafarer.*" *Neuphilologische Mitteilungen* 79 (1978): 1–6.

Page, R. I. *An Introduction to English Runes.* London: Methuen, 1973.

Parker, Roscoe E. "*Gyd, Leoð,* and *Sang* in Old English Poetry." *Tennessee Studies in Literature* 1 (1956): 59–63.

Pasternack, Carol Braun. "Stylistic Disjunctions in *The Dream of the Rood.*" *Anglo-Saxon England* 13 (1984): 167–86.

Payne, Richard C. "Convention and Originality in the Vision Framework of *The Dream of the Rood.*" *Modern Philology* 73 (1976): 329–41.

Pearsall, Derek. *Old English and Middle English Poetry.* London: Routledge, 1977.

Plato. *Phaedrus,* translated by R. Hackforth. In *Plato,* edited by Edith Hamilton and Huntington Cairns. Princeton, NJ: Princeton University Press, 1961.

Pope, John Collins. "Dramatic Voices in *The Wanderer* and *The Seafarer.*" In *Franciplegius: Medieval and Linguistic Studies in Honor of Francis P. Magoun, Jr,* edited by Jess B. Bessinger, Jr. and Robert P. Creed, 164–93. New York: New York University Press, 1965.

———. "Second Thoughts on the Interpretation of *The Seafarer.*" *Anglo-Saxon England* 3 (1974): 75–86.

Renoir, Alain. "The Least Elegiac of the Elegies: A Contextual Glance at *The Husband's Message.*" *Studia Neophilologica* 53 (1981): 69–76.

———. "A Reading Context for *The Wife's Lament.*" In *Anglo Saxon Poetry: Essays in Appreciation,* edited by Lewis E. Nicholson and Dorothy Warwick Frese, 224–41. Notre Dame, IN: University of Notre Dame Press, 1975.

Richman, Gerald. "Speakers and Speech Boundaries in *The Wanderer.*" *Journal of English and Germanic Philology* 81 (1982): 469–79.

Rissanen, Matti. "The Theme of 'Exile' in *The Wife's Lament.*" *Neuphilologische Mitteilungen* 70 (1969): 90–104.

Robertson, D. W., Jr. *A Preface to Chaucer.* Princeton NJ: Princeton University Press, 1962.

Rogers, William Elford. *The Three Genres and the Interpretation of the Lyric.* Princeton: Princeton University Press, 1983.

Rosier, James L. "The Literal-Figurative Identity of *The Wanderer.*" *PMLA* 79 (1964): 366–69.

Rumble, Thomas C. "From *Eardstapa* to *Snottor on Mode:* The Structural Principle of *The Wanderer.*" *Modern Language Quarterly* 19 (1958): 225–30.

Salmon, Vivian. " 'The Wanderer' and 'The Seafarer' and the Old English Conception of the Soul." *Modern Language Review* 55 (1960): 1–10.

Schaar, Claes. "On a New Theory of Old English Poetic Diction." *Neophilologus* 40 (1956): 301–05.

Schlauch, Margaret. "An Old English *Encomium Urbis.*" *Journal of English and Germanic Philology* 40 (1941): 14–28.

Sedgefield, Walter J. "Old English Notes." *Modern Language Review* 26 (1931): 74–75.

Shields, John C. "*The Seafarer* as a *Meditatio.*" *Studia Mystica* 3 (1980), i: 29–41.

Shippey, T. A. *Old English Verse.* London: Hutchinson University Library, 1972.

Sisam, Kenneth. "Cynewulf and His Poetry." *Proceedings of the British Academy* 18 (1932): 303–31.

———. *Studies in the History of Old English Literature.* Oxford: Oxford University Press, 1962.

Smithers, G. V. "The Meaning of *The Seafarer* and *The Wanderer.*" *Medium Ævum* 26 (1957): 137–53; 28 (1959): 1–22.

Spamer, James B. "The Marriage Concept in *Wulf and Eadwacer.*" *Neophilologus* 62 (1978): 143–44.

Spitzer, Leo. "A Note on the Poetic and Empirical 'I' in Medieval Authors." *Traditio* 4 (1946): 414–22.

Stanley, E. G. "Old English Poetic Diction and the Interpretation of *The Wanderer, The Seafarer,* and *The Penitent's Prayer.*" *Anglia* 73 (1956): 413–66.

Stevens, Martin, and Jerome Mandel, eds. *Old English Literature: Twenty-two Analytical Essays.* Lincoln: University of Nebraska Press, 1968.

Stevens, William O. *The Cross in the Life and Literature of the Anglo-Saxons.* New York: Holt, 1904.

Stevick, R[obert] D. "The Meter of *The Dream of the Rood. Neuphilologische Mitteilungen* 68 (1967): 149–68.

———. "Oral-Formulaic Analysis of Old English Verse." *Speculum* 37 (1962): 382–89.

Stewart, Ann Harleman. "Kenning and Riddle in Old English." *Papers on Language & Literature* 15 (1979): 115–36.

Stock, Brian. *The Implications of Literacy: Written Language and Models of Interpretation in the Eleventh and Twelfth Centuries.* Princeton, NJ: Princeton University Press, 1983.

Swanton, Michael J. "*The Wife's Lament* and *The Husband's Message:* A Reconsideration." *Anglia* 82 (1964): 269–90.

———, ed. *The Dream of the Rood.* Manchester, U.K.: Manchester University Press, 1970.

Timmer, B. J. "The Elegiac Mood in Old English Poetry." *English Studies* 24 (1942): 33–44.

Tripp, Raymond P. "The Narrator as Revenant: A Reconsideration of Three Old English Elegies." *Papers on Language & Literature* 8 (1972): 339–61.

Tuggle, Thomas T. "The Structure of *Deor.*" *Studies in Philology* 74 (1977): 229–42.

Tupper, Frederick, Jr. "The Cynewulfian Runes of the Religious Poems." *Modern Language Notes* 27 (1912): 131–37.

———. "Notes on Old English Poems, v: Hand ofer Heafod." *Journal of English and Germanic Philology* 11 (1912): 97–100.

Van't Hul, Bernard, and Dennis S. Mitchell. " 'Artificial Poetry' and Sea Eagles." *Neuphilologisch Mitteilungen* 81 (1980): 390–94.

Vickrey, John F. "Some Hypotheses Concerning 'The Seafarer,' Lines 1–47." *Archiv für das Studium der Neueren Sprachen und Literaturen* 219 (1982): 57–77.

Ward, J. A. "*The Wife's Lament.*" *Journal of English and Germanic Philology* 59 (1960): 26–33.

Watts, Ann Chalmers. *The Lyre and the Harp.* New Haven: Yale University Press, 1969.

Wentersdorf, Karl P. "The Situation of the Narrator in the Old English *Wife's Lament.*" *Speculum* 56 (1981): 492–516.

Whitbread, Leslie. "A Note on *Wulf and Eadwacer.*" *Medium Ævum* 10 (1941): 150–54.

Whitelock, Dorothy. *The Beginnings of English Society.* Baltimore: Penguin, 1966.

———. "The Interpretation of *The Seafarer.*" In *The Early Cultures of North-West Europe,* edited by Cyril Fox and Bruce Dickens, 259–72. Cambridge: Cambridge University Press, 1950.

Williamson, Craig. *A Feast of Creatures: Anglo-Saxon Riddle-Songs.* Philadelphia: University of Pennsylvania Press, 1982.

Woolf, Rosemary. "Doctrinal Influences on *The Dream of the Rood.*" *Medium Ævum* 27 (1958): 137–53.

———. "*The Wanderer, The Seafarer,* and the Genre of *Planctus,*" In *Anglo-Saxon Poetry: Essays in Appreciation,* edited by Lewis E. Nicholson and Dolores Warwick Frese, 192–207. Notre Dame, IN: University of Notre Dame Press, 1975.

Wrenn, C. L. *A Study of Old English Literature.* London: Haprap, 1967.

Zumthor, Paul. *Speaking of the Middle Ages,* translated by Sarah White. Lincoln: University of Nebraska Press, 1986.

Index

Adoptable speaker, 58–64
Aelfric's *Grammar and Glossary,* 59
Alcuin, 32
Aldhelm, 32; "De virginitate," 46
"Aldhelm," 46–47, 124
Alfred, 24, 32, 44, 45, 46, 113, 142 n.1
Allegory, 56, 77, 88, 93, 108, 109,
141 n.9 (chap. 2), 143 n.7, 144 n.9,
145 n.19
Alliteration. *See* Prosody
Anacoluthon, 85
Anglo-Saxon Chronicle, The, 9, 10, 66,
68, 75–76. *See also* titles of poems
Anonymous poetry, 23, 29–30, 34, 36,
140 n.9
Aphorisms, 86–87, 89, 91–92, 95–97,
99, 102, 108, 109–10, 134
Apostrophe, 58, 86, 90–91
Asser, 32
Audience, 34–36
Authors: gender of, 23, 32, 139–40 n.8;
identity of, 31–32, 45, 68–69, 75–76,
99, 113; role of, 29, 34, 37–38, 45, 46–
47
Authorship, concept of, 29, 38, 137–38.
See also Anonymous poetry; Divine
inspiration

"Battle of Brunanburh," 10, 58, 66, 71–
76, 77, 83, 139 n.7
"Battle of Maldon," 10, 66
Bede, 30, 68; *Ecclesiastical History,* 66,
113
Benedict Biscop, 32
Beowulf, 25, 31, 34, 79–83, 127, 139 nn.
3, 5, and 7; "The Father's Lament,"
20, 66, 73, 79–83; "The Last Survivor," 20, 86
Brussels Cross, 44, 122

Caedmon, 30, 31, 32, 58, 68, 83
"Caedmon's Hymn," 65, 66–67, 68, 79,
83

Canterbury Tales, 35
"Capture of the Five Boroughs," 69–
70, 71
Celtic language, 62; and literature, 143–
44 n.8; and poets, 28
Charms, 9, 21, 58–59, 61–64, 98,
142 n.2
Chaucer, 9, 20, 28, 29, 35
Christ II, 114, 117–18, 119
Closure, 69, 73
"Coronation of Edgar," 68–69, 71
Cotton Claudius A.iii, 45
Cotton Otho C.i, 44
Cotton Vitellius A.xv, 139 n.5
Cuthbert, 32, 67
Cynewulf, 9, 24, 30–31, 32, 112, 114–
20, 142 n.1. *See also* titles of poems

Dating of poems, 24, 65, 77, 122–23
"Death of Alfred," 68–69, 71
"Death of Edgar," 70–71
"Death of Edward," 68–69, 71
"Deor," 20, 85, 86–87, 89, 97–102, 109,
110, 142 n.2
Divine inspiration, 16, 30–31, 118–19
"Dream of the Rood," 9, 10, 24, 45, 54,
57, 111, 121–28
"Durham," 65, 67–68, 75, 141 n.3
(chap. 4)

Elegy, 2, 9, 10, 20, 77, 139 n.2, 142 n.10
Elene, 24, 30–31, 114, 118–20, 122, 124,
126
Empathy, 26, 49, 58, 62, 92, 95, 106,
110, 126
"Epilogue to ms. 41, Corpus Christi
College," 112–14
Epithets, 25
Ethelred, 69
Ethopoeia. *See* Fictive speaker
Exeter Book, 17, 18, 24, 28, 34, 53, 54,
60, 65, 85, 87, 139 n.5, 143 n.5,
144 n.12. *See also* titles of poems

"Fates of the Apostles," 24, 112, 114, 115–16, 118
"Father's Lament," 20, 66, 75, 79–83
Fictive speaker, 85–111, 121, 124–25, 127, 128, 138
Folklore, 93, 97, 110, 143–44 n.8. *See also* Riddles
Formulas, 25, 26
"For Unfruitful Land," 61–62
French literature, 21, 23; and poets, 21

Gerald of Wales, 27
German literature: *Frauenlied,* 20, 139 n.1; *Krist,* 115; *Nibelungenlied,* 20; *Wechsel,* 23
German poets: Hartmann von Aue, 115; der von Kurenberc, 20; *Minnesanger,* 21; Otfrid 115
Godwine, 69
Gnomes. *See* Aphorisms
Greek alphabet, 43
Greek language, 46; and literature, 25
Gregory, 46; *Dialogues,* 45; *Pastoral Care,* 46, 142 n.1

Harold Godwinsson, 69
Hrotswith, 32
"Husband's Message," 9, 20, 27, 45, 47, 53–57, 122, 124, 140–41 nn. 6–9, 144 n.9
Hygeburh, 32
Hypostatization of literature, 15–19, 28–29, 38, 113

Icelandic literature, 137, 139 n.6
Inanimate speakers, 43–57, 121–24, 126–27
Individual, concept of, 29, 118, 125, 127, 137
Inscriptions, 43–44, 122–23

John the Old Saxon, 32
"Journey Charm," 61, 62–64
Juliana, 112, 114, 116–17, 118, 119
Junius manuscript, 28

"Kentish Hymn," 65, 142 n.1

Lambeth Psalter, 59
"Last Survivor," 20, 86
Latin (in Anglo-Saxon England), 32, 44, 46, 48, 67–68, 114

Leofric, 18
Lettered composition, 24, 28, 31–32, 98, 118–20, 139 nn. 3 and 4
Life of St. Leofgyth, 32
Literacy, 24, 26, 28, 30, 31, 34, 44, 56–57, 122, 137, 138
Litotes, 61
Lives of St. Willibald and St. Wynnebald, 32
Lyric poetry: definition of, 19–24, 36–38

Macaronic verse, 46
Manuscript books, 17–19, 24, 28, 35, 44, 45, 46, 75–76. *See also* titles of books
Manuscript composition, 27
Manuscript cultures, 24, 26–29, 38, 44, 112, 140 n.9
Memorability, 25, 26, 60, 97, 139 n.4
Metaphor, 49, 50, 51, 61, 62, 64, 70, 87, 88, 89, 91, 110, 127, 133, 135, 140 n.4, 145 nn. 19 and 20
"Metrical Preface to the Pastoral Care," 46
"Metrical Preface to Waerferth's Translation of Gregory's *Dialogues,*" 45
Middle English literature, 20, 21. *See also* Chaucer
Monasteries, 28, 31–32, 70, 139 n.7, 146 n.3
Monks and nuns, 27, 32, 37
Mozarabic poetry, 20

Nature imagery, 72, 73, 75, 85–86, 89, 97, 102–4, 105–7, 109, 129–31, 133. *See also* Pathetic fallacy
Negative Capability, 33, 140 n.9
New Criticism, 29
Nonpersonal speaker, 65–84, 115–19
Norse, 98, 143 n.2, 147 n.2; Vikings, 70, 72, 143 n.2. *See also* Icelandic literature

Odoaker saga cycle, 142 n.2, 144 n.8
Offa saga cycle, 143 n.8
Oral composition, 24–26, 27, 30, 31, 37, 44, 139 n.3
Oral culture, 24–26, 56, 61, 112, 139 n.6
Oral performance, 28, 34, 38, 44
Oswy, 32

Paganism, 143 nn. 6 and 7
Pathetic fallacy, 26, 86, 90, 94, 95, 103–4, 105, 107, 109
"Penitent's Prayer," 60–61, 142 n.1
Personal poetry, 22–23, 38
Personal speaker, 44, 112–20, 121, 124–35, 138
Personification, 26, 45–57, 62–64, 76, 86, 104, 105–6, 131, 134, 147 n.4. *See also* Prosopopoeia
"Phoenix," 46
Portuguese literature, 20
"Prayer, A," 59–60
Prayers, 21, 58–61, 113, 114–17, 125, 146 n.1 (chap. 4)
Print culture, 28–29
Prosody, 20–21, 25, 99, 102, 104, 105, 118, 134
Prosopopoeia, 43–57, 122–24. *See also* Personification

Readership (as distinct from audience), 112–13, 116–20
Reading (silent, private), 28, 34, 137
Redundancy, 25, 26
"Resignation," 20, 53, 60–61, 85, 86, 87–89, 97, 102, 109. *See also* "Penitent's Prayer"
"Riddle 5," 49
"Riddle 16," 48
"Riddle 20," 50–51, 54
"Riddle 23," 47
"Riddle 25," 51
"Riddle 27," 51–52, 54
"Riddle 30b," 47, 53
"Riddle 44," 47
"Riddle 47," 47
"Riddle 60," 47, 53, 54, 140 n.6
"Riddle 66," 47–48
"Riddle 74," 52
"Riddle 77," 47
"Riddle 88," 48, 49, 51
Riddles, 9, 21, 24, 43, 44, 47–52, 53, 102, 115–16, 122, 140 nn. 3–5, 147 n.4
Rime. *See* Prosody
"Riming Poem," 20, 85, 89, 93, 102–4, 106, 110–11, 129, 135

Romantic poetry, 22, 29, 33, 137
Rudolf, 32
"Ruin," 20, 53, 65, 66, 73, 76–79, 83, 127
Runes, 55, 112, 114, 140–41 n.8, 146 n.1
Runic inscriptions, 27, 43–44, 54–57, 122–23
Ruthwell Cross, 122–23

Satire, 29
Scholastics, 29
Scops, 85, 97, 98, 100–102, 139 n.4. *See also* Oral composition; Oral performance
"Seafarer," 17, 18, 20, 25, 66, 85, 89, 93, 96, 102, 105, 111, 121, 124, 127, 129, 130
Self, concept of, 22–23, 33–34, 36, 38, 112–13, 137, 140 n.9
Solomon and Saturn, 113
Spacial point of view, 67, 75, 77–79, 142 n.12
Structure of poems, 35, 86–87, 108, 114, 129. *See also* Closure
Syntax, 25, 26

"Thureth," 45, 54, 124
Titles for poems, 17, 28–29, 35, 53, 60

Unity (as a literary principle), 34–35, 123, 127

Vercelli Book, 24, 28, 123. *See also* titles of poems
Volsungasaga, 142 n.2

Waerferth, 45, 140 n.1, 142 n.1
"Wanderer," 10, 20, 66, 89, 96, 111, 121, 128–35, 145 n.19
"Widsith," 97, 139 n.4
"Wife's Lament," 9, 20, 25, 53, 85, 87, 89, 92–97, 102, 105, 109, 124, 143–44 n.8, 145 n.19
Wolfdietrich B legend, 142 n.2
Writing, 27–28, 38, 43, 44
"Wulf and Eadwacer," 17, 20, 85, 86, 87, 89–92, 93, 97, 102, 109, 139 n.7